Honus Wagner

On His Life & Baseball

HARRY S. BRESSLER
~1914

"The Grand Old Man of Baseball" was the title given to this drawing of Honus Wagner and the photo from which it was taken. A color rendition of the same image was the cover art for the January 1915 issue of *Baseball Magazine*. The entire issue was dedicated to Wagner and was subtitled "The Hans Wagner Number." *(Baseball Magazine)*

Honus Wagner

On His Life & Baseball

William R. Cobb, Editor

All inquiries should be addressed to:
Sports Media Group
An imprint of Ann Arbor Media Group, LLC
2500 S. State Street
Ann Arbor, MI 48104

Library of Congress Cataloging-in-Publication Data

Wagner, Honus, 1874-1955.
  Honus wagner : a self-portrait / William R. Cobb, Editor.
     p. cm.
  ISBN-13: 978-1-58726-308-8 (hardcover : alk. paper)
  ISBN-10: 1-58726-308-4 (hardcover : alk. paper)
  1. Wagner, Honus, 1874-1955. 2. Baseball players–United States–Biography.
  3. Pittsburgh Pirates (Baseball team) I. Cobb, William R. II. Title.

GV865.W33A3 2006
796.357092–dc22

Printed and bound in the United States of America.

10 09 08 07 06   1 2 3

CONTENTS

FOREWORD

At the time Wagner wrote these newspaper articles, his only auto-biographical work, he was six years beyond his playing days with Pittsburgh, but baseball was still a major part of his life. After shunning most public appearances during his playing career, Wagner had become a sought after speaker at civic and sports events. As perhaps the most famous player in the major leagues, and certainly around the Pittsburgh area, he quickly became a darling of the local speaker's circuit. By 1924 he was comfortable in the spotlight as a public speaker, and had grown to thoroughly enjoy the reaction of his audiences to his anecdotes and his sometimes embellished tales of the diamond. In the later years of his life, Wagner developed a reputation for making up outlandish and even unbelievable stories to capture the attention of his audience. The stories in this autobiographical work seem not to fall into that category, however, the timing being a decade or so before Wagner's wild creativity in storytelling reached full bloom.

Questions naturally arise about a work such as this when it is published so long after the original publication, and when the author is no longer around to answer questions or clarify for inquisitive readers. The question of actual authorship is usually the first to be asked. The use of ghostwriters was seriously frowned upon in the early part of the twentieth century. A scandal in the early part of that century led to the Baseball Commissioner prohibiting star players from lending their name to any work that they did not actually write.

Another question that must be asked of this autobiography concerns the accuracy of what Wagner has presented in these chapters. There is clear evidence that there were no professional fact-checkers used when these articles were published. Even the date of Wagner's first professional baseball contract is in error by two years, if one is to believe a partial copy of that contract published nine years earlier in *Baseball Magazine*. Given this glaring error alone, the editor cautions the reader that details, including such things as game dates, batting averages and box scores, should not be relied upon without some corroborating information.

The final question asked about works such as this relates to truthfulness. Wagner recounts that he resorted to batting left-handed against Jack Taylor, who played for Chicago and St. Louis. Wagner identified Taylor as the most difficult pitcher for him to hit. He then categorically states that he never again batted left-handed. This being true, Wagner would not have batted left-handed after Taylor's 1907 retirement. Nevertheless, a photo showing Wagner batting left-handed against the Giants in 1908 has recently been discovered and verified. Could this be deceit, or maybe just forgetfulness? Surely not deceit. Quite possibly forgetfulness. Or, perhaps, it represents the early beginning of Wagner's penchant for storytelling. Certainly, this anecdote about a one-time left-handed at-bat fit well into the flow of the story line as presented by Wagner, and it answered a question he had received from an admiring fan.

In these pages, Wagner comes across as a genuine, down-home philosopher with deep love for the game of baseball, and for other sports as well. The text reads much like a dictated conversation, replete with exclamations like "Gee!" "How about that!" and "Believe Me!"—a Wagner standard. The editor feels that Wagner most likely penned this work on his own. Certainly not without editorial assistance that would accompany any widely printed article, but quite possibly without a major influence by what would now be considered a ghostwriter.

The following introductory paragraph, which preceded most of the published chapters in the *Los Angeles Times*, was written by an insightful and competent editor—and an obviously admiring fan. It captures the essence of this unique and historical glimpse into the life of one of baseball's greatest players.

"Hans Wagner's name appears on every All-American all-star baseball team for all time, and what the old-time star doesn't know about baseball doesn't amount to much. In this, the story of his career told by himself, he tells you what he knows—the skill of men and teams and plays, the development of the American game, all the ins and outs that the baseball fan of today wants to know about. He gives pointers to the youngster and the college player, and he tells the old hand where he can look for new delights by watching for fine points that most of us overlook.

Hans Wagner's story is more than this, however; to it he has brought his sound philosophy and knowledge of men, so that the diamond, as he talks of it, becomes as broad as the whole world. And with a simplicity that makes absorbing reading, he has accomplished what many skilled writers fail to achieve; he has given a living, full-length portrait of a man—himself."

Editor's Notes

This autobiography appeared serially as "Hans Wagner's Story" in the *Los Angeles Times* from December 13, 1923 through January 23, 1924. It was syndicated by the North American Newspaper Alliance. It also appeared in the *Pittsburgh Gazette Times* under a slightly different title in January and February of 1924.

The text for this edition was retyped from printed microfilm images of eighty-year-old *Los Angeles Times* issues. The quality and legibility of these printed images were poor. Many words could barely be read at all and could only be deciphered with a good understanding of the context. I have gone to great lengths to check and recheck the transcription and feel confident that its accuracy is very high.

The *Pittsburgh Gazette Times* was used as the source for chapters that were, for reasons unknown, never printed by the *Los Angeles Times*.

Names and places have been verified to the extent possible and explained by footnotes where clarification seemed to be in order. Original chapter titles and subtitles have been used although they are likely the work of newspaper editors and not Honus Wagner. Archaic spelling and word usage have been modernized to improve the flow to the modern reader. However, extensive changes were not required to achieve this modernization. Every attempt has been made to retain the colloquial flavor of Wagner's words and to preserve the overall sense in the text that this story is actually Honus Wagner's story—and seemingly not that of an unknown ghostwriter.

The support and assistance of the Sports Media Group staff and the talent and cooperation of Andy Amato in producing the cover image are greatly appreciated.

I've Never Quit the Game

• • •

When I first talked with the publisher about this series of baseball articles—my autobiography, he called it—I was much in doubt, and still am, as to what people might want to know about me.

"Why," he said, "in the first place, thousands of fans would like to know what you are doing now." Then he stopped.

"And," he went on again, "they certainly would like to know what made you a great ball player, and so on."

"A thing that has always puzzled me," he added, "is why you had to quit playing—why you dropped out of the game."

"But I haven't quit the game," I told him. "I play ball two or three times a week right now"—this was in September—"and I make a pretty good living out of it."

"Well, start right there," he suggested. "By the way, Honus, how old are you?—And another thing, a lot of folks think you talk with a German accent—were you born in this country?"

I'll answer all that at one time. I am 49 years old. I was born in Mansfield, Pennsylvania, which is now called Carnegie. Of course, I never had a German dialect. Moreover, my name is John Peter—not Hans or Honus. Those were given me as nicknames. I went to school, just the same as the other boys—and I don't even speak German well. My father, though, was born in the old country. He came here when a young man and went to work as a coal miner in the hard coal fields.

STILL PLAYS REGULARLY

Though I am 49 years of age I play baseball regularly, and I don't mind telling you I play a pretty good game yet. I don't feel a year older than I did when I was leading the National League as a batter with the Pittsburgh club. I play with a semipro team in summer and often get in as many as four games a week. In addition to

1

that I have a sporting goods business which I help my partners attend to between times.

I play ball simply because I like to. I have never gotten tired of the game. As a rule ball players who like to quit the game and forget about it never were really great players. To be successful in baseball a man has got to feel it. The game must be in his bones. He must love it. It's just the same as any other business. I don't believe a man ever made a great success of any business that he didn't really love.

You may be surprised when I tell you that I never thought of quitting baseball as a game and, what's more, that never in my life did I pay much attention to the money end of it.

Any man who succeeds in making himself the best in his trade has earned a place in life and his name will be remembered.

To say that baseball is a useless profession would be as much as saying that the 60,000 people who went out to see a game during the last world's series were all fools. A man who can do something

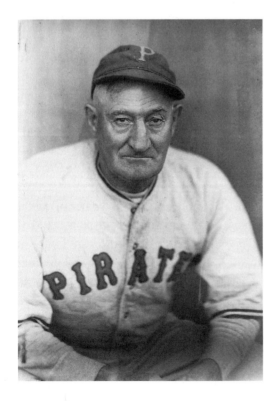

Honus Wagner takes in a game from the dugout in this 1930s photo. (George Brace Photo Collection)

to entertain and hold the interest of 60,000 people at one place, and a million more scattered over the country, has made a successful mark in life—make no mistake about that.

NEVER TIRES OF BASEBALL

I did not drop out of major league baseball because I was all through. I was not released. There was a contract on the table for me to sign at increased salary. As I say, I never paid much attention to the money end. I wanted to stay at home for a while. I had traveled around from city to city for twenty-eight years and was weary of it—the traveling, I mean. I was never tired of baseball.

"No," I finally said to Mr. Dreyfuss.* "I think I'll quit. I want to be at home with my family."

He knew that I meant it. He also knew that I was not after more money. He knew that on two or three occasions I had voluntarily cut my own salary.

Though I am jumping into the middle of my story right at the start, some fans may be interested to know that I lost $2,500 out of my own pocket, and maybe more, by declining to jump to the American League during the big baseball war twenty years ago. I also knew exactly what I was doing, and I have never regretted it.

There has been much talk and misunderstanding about that incident, so, before going back to my start, I will explain the whole thing in detail.

• • •

*Barney Dreyfuss (1865–1932). Born Bernhard Dreifus in Germany, he came to the United States in 1881 at the age of fifteen and settled in Kentucky. He did well in the family liquor business and soon became part owner of the Louisville Colonels. In 1899 he bought the Pittsburgh Pirates, which he managed. He also assumed the business aspects of the team and scouted for new players. When the National League was reduced from twelve to eight teams in 1900, Dreyfuss moved the entire Louisville team to Pittsburgh. In 1903, after winning the National League pennant three years in a row, Dreyfuss proposed that his National League winners play the American League winners in a play-off series. This became an American tradition known today as the World Series. In 1909 Dreyfuss built Forbes Field in Pittsburgh, the first modern baseball park capable of seating 25,000 fans.

Why I Asked for a Smaller Salary

• • •

The big turning point in baseball, the way I look at it, was the war with the American League back in 1900, which lasted for two or three years and then wound up in the present national agreement.

That war was to baseball much like the Civil War was to the states, it had to come to a head some time. It worked a lot of hardships one way and another, but I think it was necessary.

Baseball would not have been what it is today if we hadn't had this war. We wouldn't have had any world's series for one thing. Can you imagine what baseball would be today if we didn't have a world's series as a sort of big climax to the end of the season?

In the old days a team won the pennant and the players were paid off and given a banquet. That's all there was to it. I didn't even go to the public banquets. There was nothing to talk about during the winter. Often fans forgot who had won the pennant the year before. It didn't make any difference.

That thing of having a big classic event to end the season, a climax, gave baseball its big jump. Every fall and winter the series is talked about all over the world. Now fans in little towns know all about each player and what he did. In the old days they wouldn't even know who won the pennant and wouldn't care. You know how it is.

Well it was during that war that I came into prominence in money matters—baseball money, I mean. I was among those players who refused to jump. I may have lost a lot of money by it, but I feel much happier and satisfied for having stayed in Pittsburgh.

My friends, good ball players all over the country were going to the American League for the big money. Naturally, a lot of agents, most of them friends, were after me. I was leading the National League as a hitter and, if I do say it myself, was supposed to be a good drawing card. I loved my team and associations. They meant much more to me than money.

PLAYERS TAKE A STAND

One day the players had a meeting to talk about the offers they had had and to decide what they should do. After a lot of talk we agreed to meet again the next day at 3 o'clock and not to sign a contract until after that meeting.

Mr. Dreyfuss and Harry Pulliam,* who was then with the Pittsburgh club but later president of the National League, got wind of this in some way. They knew, of course, that American League agents were in town. They tried to get hold of me but I avoided them.

On the day before the meeting my friend Jim Orris, a lifelong pal, came out to see me and finally got me to meet Dreyfuss and Pulliam in the office. Jim didn't say so, but I knew they had got him to try and get me in tow. The upshot of it was that I finally agreed to do what Jim asked. We met Dreyfuss and Pulliam at the time and place. They persuaded Orris to sit in at the conference.

They had prepared two or three contracts and tried their best to get me to sign one. I couldn't do that because I was under promise, and I didn't want them to know this. I shifted around and evaded questions—did everything I could to keep from giving a direct answer. In short, I refused to sign any form of contract.

Barney Dreyfuss is a square fellow—always treated me right. He was puzzled at my attitude.

Finally he turned to his desk and pulled a blank contract out of the drawer. For some time he looked me squarely in the eye.

• • •

*Harry Pulliam (1869–1909). Harry Pulliam was a newspaper editor when he was hired by Barney Dreyfuss to be secretary for the Louisville team, and then followed Dreyfuss to Pittsburgh in 1900. Later, as president of the National League when the American League was in formation, he oversaw development of the working agreement between leagues that lasted for decades. Known as an idealist and as a fearless and honest leader, Pulliam had personal difficulty coping with criticism, including that arising from the Merkle incident in 1908. After an extended leave of absence early in 1909, he committed suicide on July 25, 1909.

"Here Honus," he said, "is a blank contract. Take that pen there and write in your own figures."

To prove that he meant it, Barney signed the paper in blank and passed it over to me. Now that's what I call a square proposition. Still, I hesitated.

"No," I finally told them all. "I'll not sign a contract tonight no matter how it's made out. I simply can't, that's all."

It was about midnight by this time. Dreyfuss and Pulliam went out and left me with Orris, leaving it to him to do what he could with me.

"Honus," said Orris, "what did the American League offer you?"

"They offered me a two-year contract at $7500, and put the money up in the bank in advance."

I had also been offered $2,000 for each star player I could induce to go along with me.

"All right," he said, encouraged. "We'll tell Barney about that in the morning and I know he'll do the same."

"No," I told him, "I'm not worth that much money now. I think, though, Barney ought to pay me $5,000. I'm getting $4,000 now."

Barney Dreyfuss was part owner of the Louisville Colonels and in 1899 he bought the Pittsburgh Pirates, which he managed. In 1900, Dreyfuss moved the entire Louisville team to Pittsburgh and managed them until 1930. In 1903, after winning the National League pennant three years in a row, Dreyfuss proposed that his National League winners play the American League winners in a play-off series. This became an American tradition known today as the World Series. In 1909, Dreyfuss built Forbes Field in Pittsburgh, the first modern baseball park capable of seating 25,000 fans. (National Baseball Hall of Fame Library, Cooperstown, New York)

"That's fine. He'll gladly do that. Come on and sign it tonight."

"No, Jim, to tell you the truth, the fellows had a meeting and all agreed not to sign anything until we meet again tomorrow."

Orris went in to see Dreyfuss again. He came back with contracts showing that several of the fellows already had signed.

"Even so," I told them, "that's no reason why I should break my word. I won't sign tonight."

That ended the meeting.

The next day I signed the contract, and I signed it for less than $7,500. I honestly didn't think I was worth that much. Later on I was the highest paid player in the league, getting $10,000.

I'm not trying to make myself a moral hero or anything like that, but I'm telling you honestly that it was worth that $2,500 to have had the feeling of keeping my word.

There was a time though when I tried to hold a manager up for more money. That was many, many years ago. To tell it will take me right back to my beginning as a funny little awkward kid.

Harry Pulliam was club secretary for the Louisville Colonels and moved with the team to Pittsburgh in 1900. He was elected as National League president in 1903 and helped forge a peace with the upstart American League. He was strongly criticized over ruling the game a tie after the 1908 Merkle "bonehead" incident. Shortly afterward, he suffered a mental breakdown and took an extended leave of absence in early 1909. Pulliam later returned to work but remained depressed, committing suicide on July 25, 1909. (National Baseball Hall of Fame Library, Cooperstown, New York)

I Ask $40 a Month and Change My Mind

• • •

My baseball career really began at the age of 14. Even at that age I could hit the ball. For that reason I was allowed to play on the town team with boys of 18 and 19. My natural love for the game probably kept me from being a very good barber.

I belonged to one of those families where the boys are supposed to learn a trade and make their own living. My brother had a barber shop in Mansfield, which later became Carnegie, and I went to work for him as an apprentice. My job was to keep things straightened up, dust off the customers and run errands. On Saturday afternoon and night, I was allowed to do a little shaving. Many a big miner has suffered at my hands. There weren't many tips in those days.

The only thing in the way of a great barber future for me was my desire to play baseball. I played on the town team and

you can bet I never allowed plain or fancy barbering to interfere much with my pitching. Yes, I started out as a pitcher. Most ball players do, I find. Mike Donlin and Cy Seymour, you know, started out as pitchers. Every Saturday afternoon the boys used to come around in front of the barber shop and tip me off that a game was on. I would immediately duck the job. That night, though, I would come back and finish up at the shop.

My brother didn't like this a bit. He used to tell me that I'd have to stop so much ball playing or I would never make a good barber. I guess he was right. He fired me several times, but, of course, when we got home and talked it over with my dad he would take me back. There had to come a break.

One afternoon I was given the job of shaving an old miner who had a beard like a shoebrush. He didn't care who shaved him. I went to work on him and got him all lathered up and ready. I had just shaved down one side and around to his chin when one of the gang whistled outside. I sneaked out.

Who Shaved Other Half?

"You got to pitch a great game today," one of the boys told me. "If we win we're going to get new uniforms with letters on 'em."

I forgot all about my miner sitting in the chair, half-shaved and asleep. I never went back. My career as a barber was ended.

"I can stand for just so much," my brother told me that night, "and no more. You are through as a barber."

I was tickled over that. I knew I could get a job in the mines working on the trap door for my dad. This is no place to explain mining but any man in the hard- or soft-coal fields knows what a trap door boy is.* Anyway, I worked at that awhile, playing baseball in between times.

John S. Robb, Jr.,† now a prominent citizen of Pittsburgh, was captain of the Mansfield team and gave me a regular job. We played in what was the Allegheny County League, made up of Mansfield, Bridgeville, Tarentum and the Our Boys Club of Pittsburgh. The players were mostly amateurs. Shad Gwilliam was manager.

I started playing shortstop then and got $5 a week for two games. I played around that way, doing the best I could between working in the mines and playing baseball for two or three years—just like other boys might do.

• • •

*A trap door, or weather door, in a mine passage was used to regulate or direct the ventilating air current. The apprentice employee hired to open and close these mine doors was typically called a "trap door boy," or sometimes a "trapper boy" or simply a "trapper."

†John S. Robb, Jr., later a prominent Pittsburgh attorney and Life Board Member of the first Carnegie Free Library, provided Wagner's first chance to play league ball. After Robb had injured his ankle playing second base, Wagner was called from the crowd as a substitute. Wagner played shortstop wearing Robb's shoes, three sizes too big, and the spectators derided "the kid." By day's end, however, his spectacular play had landed him a job with the team at $3 to $5 a game.

And right here is a good chance for me to answer a question as to my opinion on the relative merit of ball players in those days and now. You will notice that I had been a pitcher and catcher before I was sixteen.

There are just as great ball players now as there ever were. I don't believe, though, that there are as many good ones in proportion to the number playing. The reason for that is that ball playing has become highly specialized, just as the medical and dental professions have. In those days, for instance, a ball player could play most any position. I have played every position on a ball club professionally.

NO PINCH-HITTERS THEN

In those days we had never heard of a special batter to hit right-handed pitching and another to hit left-handers. The pinch-hitter was not known then. If the man whose time it was at bat couldn't deliver the necessary pinch-hit we simply let it go at that. We had no substitutes or utility men. If a man sat on the bench to be used in case of emergency, it was simply because we liked him or he had a glove, a bat or something that we wanted to use.

My brother Al was a good ball player, though a lot of fans seem to have forgotten it. He was really my first teacher. Al played on two or three different teams in the big league later. His best work was as an infielder for Washington and Brooklyn.*

In digging up the past dope, my early days seemed to be all mixed up. That is because I often played under the name of Al and that of William, my other brother. When he had a job and couldn't fill it, I was frequently sent as a substitute. That mixing up of names is to blame for there being doubt about the very early records.

In my next article I am going to give a copy of my first contract and you may be puzzled to know why it is not signed in my name. I signed William's name because he was supposed to be the man they wanted. Earning $5 or $10 in those days was quite a big event, and

• • •

*Albert "Butts" Wagner (1871–1928) played only one year in the National League, 1898, appearing as both infielder and outfielder in 63 games with the Washington Senators and 11 games with the Brooklyn Bridegrooms. In 261 plate appearances he batted .226, with 34 RBIs and 1 homerun.

you can bet we worked all kinds of schemes to do it. Jumping from one club to another didn't mean anything.

One day, while playing under the name of William, I hit a home run. The same day I played a great game at shortstop. A fellow saw me and began talking among the boys about getting "that fellow William Wagner" to play in a little league.

Up to that time I had never thought about league baseball. We didn't read the papers then like the boys do now. Even if we had we couldn't have got all the dope that we do now. The sporting pages have developed just like baseball has. Since I come to think of it, I don't remember ever hearing about a regular sporting writer, a man who did it for a living, until I got in the big league. Even then I didn't see much of them. We depended on ourselves for what we knew about baseball. There wasn't very much to read.

He Dodged the Banquets

Often I have been asked why it is that I never got in the papers much—never was interviewed. The reason is that I always avoided reporters. It wasn't because I didn't like them, but I am naturally timid that way. I was always frightened at being interviewed and I was just as bad about going to banquets and big parties. I would slip away from them every chance I got.

A young fellow did interview me once when I didn't know it. He asked me who was the toughest pitcher I ever faced. I thought he was just a friend of the gang and told him that I never had seen a pitcher who wasn't tough. "They're all tough, son," I said. He made quite a piece about that in the paper.

The man who got interested in my boyhood playing around Pittsburgh was George Moreland,* later a baseball statistician. He was interested in the Tri-State League. A few days later I got a telegram from him saying he was managing the Steubenville club and wanted me—thinking my name was Al. That was the first telegram I ever

• • •

*George Leonard Moreland (1852–ca. 1933) was a sportswriter for the *Pittsburgh Post* and a founding member of the Baseball Writers Association of America in 1908. He published baseball's first comprehensive history and record book with the lengthy title: *Balldom, the Britannica of Baseball* got in my life and it caused a lot of excitement in me and among the fellows.

The telegram offered me $35 a month and my board while on the road.

That's when I made my only attempt in my whole career to be a businessman.

"If he wants you that bad," one of the fellows said, "you ought to make him pay more. He'd pay $40, if he had to."

We discussed the matter some time. Finally I made my decision. It was a big one for me, too. I sat down and with great pains wrote out a telegram.

"I can't come for less than $40 a month," I wired back.

I couldn't sleep that night while waiting for the answer.

•••••••••

... A Complete History of the American and National Leagues. First and Only Authentic Chronology Ever Published. Voluminous Records and Accurate Statistics: 1845–1914 [Youngstown, Ohio, Balldom Publishing Co., ca. 1914– v. illus., tables]. Moreland was an early baseball statistician with his own bureau. He managed the Canton, Ohio, team in the Tri-State League in 1890, and was later involved with the Louisville club. He also organized the Inter-State League in 1894.

Al Wagner vs. Al Wagner

• • •

All during the night while awaiting an answer to my telegram demanding $40 a month for my first league job, I repeated the words over and over again. My courage in demanding too much sort of scared me.

"I can't come for less than forty a month," I would repeat and wonder if I had done the right thing.

The answer came in the morning. It was simple and direct.

"If you can't accept thirty-five," it read, "you had better stay at home."

I went right up stairs, packed my little things and caught the last train. I'd take no more chances on losing that thirty-five a month. Gee, how mad I was at those fellows who had advised me to hold out! I wanted to get to Steubenville before the manager changed his mind.

Arriving at Steubenville, I looked up George Moreland and immediately signed the contract. I found it the other day hanging up in the library of the Elks' Club. It was torn in half but here it is:

STEUBENVILLE BASEBALL CLUB

Interstate League

Geo. L. Moreland, Manager

Season of 1895

Sec. 1—This is to certify that I, William Wagner, have agreed to play in the Steubenville Baseball Club during the season of 1895 at ($35) thirty-five, payable on the first and fifteenth of each month or as soon as possible.

Sec. 2—In signing to play for the Steubenville team I agree to abide by all the rules and regulations.

Sec. 3—I also agree that should my services not be agreeable to the said club the management reserves the right to release me.

Sec. 4—I agree to pay for my own uniform and shoes, the cost of same to be taken out of my first pay.

Sec. 5—I agree to report on the date notified by the manager in good condition to play ball.

13

Sec. 6—The manager of the Steubenville team to pay all my expenses while away from home.

Sec. 7—I also agree to always keep myself in good condition and should I fail to abide by all rules, all agreements between myself and the Steubenville Club shall be declared void.

Signed—William Wagner

Witness—Patrick (Patsy) Flaherty

◁STEUBENVILLE BASE BAI
Inter State League.

Season of 1895.   Geo, Io.

Sec. 1—This is to certify that I, _William Wagn_

have agreed to play in the Steubenville Base Ball Club during the s
$ 35. Unit; Fur payable on the first and fifteenth of each mo
as possible.

Sec. 2—In signing to play for the Steubenville team I agree to abide by all the

Sec. 3—I also agree that should my services not be agreeable to the said club th
to release me.

Sec. 4—I agree to pay for my own uniform and shoes, the cost of same to be tak

Sec. 5—I agree to report on the date notified by the Manager in good condition a

Sec. 6—The Manager of the Steubenville team to pay all my expenses while away

Sec. 7—I also agree to always keep myself in good condition and should I fail t
rules, all agreements between myself and said Steubenville Club shall b

Signed _William Wagner_

Wittness _Patrick Flaherty_

Honus Wagner's first baseball contract with the Steubenville Ball Club managed by George L. Moreland, as it appeared in the January 1915 issue of *Baseball Magazine*. The original document, partially mutilated, was reconstructed by Wagner in his own handwriting. He also noted that he played under the name of William Wagner for the year 1895. Note that the year of this document, 1895, differs from the year 1897 in Wagner's transcription of the same document in the text of this autobiography.
(Baseball Magazine)

Patsy Flaherty was a child-hood friend and neighbor who played ball with Honus Wagner before they made the Major Leagues. Patsy was a witness to Wagner's Steubenville contract. Flaherty played for 11 years in the Major Leagues as pitcher and sometimes outfielder with six different teams. He was a twenty-game winner in 1904, his only winning season, and in 1907 became the first National League pitcher to hit a Grand Slam home run. (George Brace Photo Collection)

You will notice this contract was not signed by the ball club. They didn't bother about little things like that in those days. In fact, I don't know why a contract was necessary. They could fire me whenever they wanted to anyway. The part that always gave me a laugh is that pay on the first and fifteenth of each month or "as soon as possible."

But those boys knew what they were doing. It never did become possible. The league broke up in two months.

Another funny clause is that one about taking out the money for my uniform and shoes the first month. You may not know it, but that clause still sticks in baseball contracts. It is obsolete, though. The big league teams never make a ball player pay for his uniform as a rule. They have a right to, just the same.

Two Break-Ups

My brother Al was also on that team. He played the infield. I was a pitcher. On that same team were two great ball players who afterward played with me in the big league. They were Claude Ritchie, the second baseman of the Pirates later, and Harry Smith, the old catcher.

When the break-up came the Steubenville team moved to Akron, Ohio, where we played on the Butchel College grounds. There we lasted just three days when the club broke up again. It seemed like I never would get that $35 coming regularly.

But there were big doings in the three days we lasted. The Wagner brothers got two home runs each day. Still, Al was the most famous.

"Honus," Al said to me as the team broke up, "I've got a job offered me at Mansfield, Ohio. I've just agreed to take one at Canton."

"Which one you want me to take?" I asked, knowing what he meant.

"As I am going to Canton you'd better take that job down at Mansfield and play as Al. We got to hold both those jobs."

The thought of doing anything wrong never entered our heads. They did all kinds of things like that then.

So I went to Mansfield and stayed a month. I played good baseball, too. All around town they were talking about that fellow, Al Wagner, having a chance to be a great ball player. Everything would have been all right, at that, I reckon, if we hadn't forgot to figure on what we would do when Canton came down to play Mansfield.

Then They Both Showed Up

There was a lot of trouble and mix-ups about Al Wagner when Canton and Mansfield hooked up. Each team had what was supposed to be the same Al Wagner. When it developed that Mansfield and Canton both had one, each crowd claimed their Wagner as the real one. We had to do all kinds of explaining. It so happened that we both played well and we were allowed to get away with the deception. I forgot to say I played third base for the Mansfield club and was throwing so hard I almost knocked down the first baseman.

All this time I was studying baseball hard. The players used to

Honus's brother Al Wagner was a solid minor league player, but he lacked the discipline to abide by the strict rules for Major League ballplayers of the era. Some fans observed that Al was a better player than Honus in the early years, but his only Major League stint in 1898 was not remarkable. Al was also Honus's best friend, hunting buddy, and basketball teammate. (George Brace Photo Collection)

wonder how a kid like me could remember the faults of all the different players. I also remembered my own faults. Often I would go out in the morning and practice to overcome these faults and also to try and imitate some good player I had seen.

The manager and owner noticed that I was studying the game seriously. Remember, I wasn't quite 21 yet.

At the end of the month—the time when I really got my pay—the owner sent me up to Adrian, Michigan, to manage a team. He had asked who would like to manage a ball club and, of course, I figured it out that such a job would just suit me. The owner was Mr. Taylor, a hardware man. I understand he has been very successful since.

This Adrian team was in the Michigan State League.

As a young manager I lasted three weeks. I had all kinds of trouble. In the first place I found the pitchers were not so good, or rather that they did not have their heart in their work.

We had a negro pitcher who had a lot of stuff. The other pitchers wanted him fired, but he was the only one who could win for me. The others all claimed to have sore arms and all such alibis as that. They were trying a run a sort of boycott.

A Cure for Sore Arms

I wanted to win those ball games and as the colored boy was the only one to do the pitching, I sent him in. He won, too. In a few days the others gradually lost their sore arms and came back one at a time.

I reckon I was a little too young to be a manager. I worried a right smart about my responsibilities. At the end of three weeks I got mighty homesick. I just couldn't stand to be away off there by myself. I moped around and after awhile was really sick, you don't know how terrible the feeling is.

Finally I decided I couldn't stand it any longer and went to join my brother Al. He was glad to see me, of course. Gee, you don't know how I perked up.

Right away Al got busy and figured out a job. He sent me to the Warren, Pennsylvania, team of the Iron and Oil League. Again I signed a contract for $35 a month and my board while away from home.

I was getting to be a pretty good ball player by this time. It was really the beginning of my career. That Warren club turned out the greatest number of players for the big league of any team in all baseball history.

On that team with me were those who afterward played in the major league:

Joe Rickert, Boston; Harry Smith, Pittsburgh; Al Wagner, Brooklyn; Claude Ritchie, Pittsburgh; Bill Carrick, New York. There were one or two others whose names I can't remember.

That will illustrate what I meant when I said there were more great players in proportion to the number engaged than there are today. Just think of that many ball players jumping direct from a little bush team right into the big league—yes, and making good, every one of them!

Sizing Up the Players

• • •

When I first began to win my spurs as a young bush league ball player I made it a point, as I have said, to watch some good player closely and try to imitate him. This, I think, would be a great help to any youngster. In trying to copy the star's fine points you will naturally discover his weak points. That proves a double benefit.

I used to watch the Baltimore Orioles whenever I had a chance, even before I got in the big league. That was a mighty tough outfit to beat. Every one of them fought to win all the time. I don't believe any one of them had a thought of how much money they were making when they got on the field. Their minds were on winning that particular ball game for their own satisfaction, as well as for the public. That is what made the Orioles so famous.

The one man I particularly watched was John McGraw. I made up my mind that I wanted to be a ball player like McGraw.

I may make you smile to think of me trying to copy McGraw. He was a little bit of a shaver, weighing about 140 pounds, while I was a big gangling fellow, weighing up around 185. Still, I admired the way he fought for every point.

I don't believe there ever lived a ball player who was McGraw's equal in getting on base, whether it was walking, being hit by the pitcher, bunting or hitting the ball out. He was likely to do either. Anyway, he nearly always got on the base.

McGraw never gave anybody any more of the base than he had to. He and Fred Clarke were tough birds when it came to taking all the bag to themselves and letting the other fellow shuffle around the best he could. The polite ball player of today often gives the base runner half of the bag to touch. Not in those days. You were lucky if you didn't get bumped into the outfield.

When McGraw was writing his "Thirty Years in Baseball" I

notice he didn't say anything about how tough that bunch made it for a fellow trying to go round that infield on a long hit. I didn't expect him to. Honestly, those fellows fought a fellow off so hard that I have actually been stuck with a horseshoe nail in passing second.

RUBBER SPIKES NOT WORN

They had a way of bumping a runner around so that a green man would often be thrown out on what might have been a home run. Mind you, that wasn't considered unsportsmanlike. It was looked on as good baseball. It was the kind of baseball that wins, too. They were not the only ones. We all went at the game pretty rough.

I hit a long drive one day at Baltimore and when I got to first base John Doyle almost bumped me into right field, pretending that he was trying to get out of the way. Stumbling to my feet I went on to second and there Jennings backed into me, bumping me into center. I kept going, though. When I started to round third McGraw snatched me by the belt. Let me tell you, that infield was tough picking.

McGraw had another trick of catching a runner by the belt and yanking him back just as he was about to score on a long fly. The umpire, you see, would be watching the ball to see just when it was caught. At that moment McGraw, with his fingers in the runner's belt, would give a jerk and stumble him a couple of steps. Often he would be checked just enough to get thrown out at the plate.

Everybody hollered and wrangled about this, but as the umpire could never see McGraw get in his fine work he would get away with it.

One day we had a big fellow on third. I can't just remember his name but he talked with a little accent—Swedish, I think. Any way, he was on third ready to score on a long fly. Like the rest of us he was onto McGraw's trick. It looked to us as if this fellow had forgotten. Surely, he paid no attention to McGraw.

The batter drove a long fly to right field. The umpire watched the catch. Our man started for the plate without even looking around. He was laughing as he slid into the plate and scored.

MCGRAW CAUGHT WITH GOODS

Then we all looked around and there was McGraw standing at third with the runner's belt in his hand. That big Swede, knowing the trick, had unfastened his belt so that it would come off when pulled. The gang didn't forget that for a long time. I'll bet McGraw hasn't forgotten it to this day.

Yes, I always regarded McGraw as a wonderful, winning ball player. I may not have copied his fielding style but I certainly picked up a lot of tricks by watching him all the time. I enjoyed reading his "Thirty Years in Baseball" because I was mixed up in many of the things he wrote about.

I may be a little ahead of my story but I want to explain right here that there is a lot of difference between throwing your whole soul into a ball game and in stopping to think about whether a thing is sportsmanlike or not. As I grow older I naturally think more of what we call sportsmanship than I did then. I'd like for all the boys to grow up as sportsmen. But when I talk about great ball players, as I will in the future chapters, I mean ball players who could win ball games. We played according to our own code then. It was just as fair for one as for the other. Nobody ever became enemies over it.

It used to be a very common thing for some runner on first base to yell down at me: "Hey, you big Dutchman, you'd better get out of the way down there or I'll cut your legs off. Watch out, I'm coming in a minute!"

"All right come on, old timer," I'd yell back at him. "The old Dutchman 'll be down here waiting."*

• • •

*There is a persistent story about a very similar incident with Ty Cobb in the 1909 world's series. In a 1951 interview with Idaho sportscaster Joe Clement, Cobb denied this story and proclaimed his longstanding friendship and respect for Wagner. Cobb labeled this story, and several other myths about him, as "Rainy Day Stories" made up by sportswriters who needed stories when games were rained out.

And don't you think they wouldn't come, either! Down they'd come with spikes flying high. I'd get 'em though.

I've got a lot of scars from spike cuts but there wasn't a one of those boys who ever meant harm in that. They meant nothing at all by it, except just talk. They just wanted to win, that's all. If they cut me I'd take it and grin. If I cut into one of them they'd take it just the same. It was all in the game.

THEY MEANT NO HARM

What I mean to say, though, is that I never saw a ball player deliberately try to injure another. I don't believe they would do it. It happened, of course, but no real harm was intended.

But to get back to those last days with the Warren team of the Iron and Oil League. I didn't realize it then but that was to be my last engagement with a minor league. Up to that time I had not thought of getting into real fast company. I was just beginning to realize how much there was to learn in baseball.

I have been credited with being a good base runner. At that time I really was as good a man on the bases as we had on the team. It wasn't so much on account of speed as of watching opponents and taking advantage of mistakes. A player can do this just as well on the bench as on the bases. Though my mind was young, I realize now that I had the faculty of not getting lost in enthusiasm and of sizing up both sides of a situation while the other fellows were all excited.

Those minor league youngsters were not as cautious as big leaguers are in their movements. It was easy to tell what they intended to do by the way they handled themselves, moved their arms, feet or legs.

Most any pitcher, until he learns by experience, will make some little motion or take some kind of a stand that will show when he is going to throw to first base or the plate, for instance.

By watching them close I could get onto this. When I felt sure the throw would be made to the plate I could take a big lead off first and steal. Base stealing, you know, is entirely a matter of the lead. It doesn't make any difference how fast a man is he can't steal second unless he gets a big lead.

When I would spot a pitcher's weakness in that respect I would tip the other fellows off. Soon we would be running wild on him and he never knew why.

There are pitchers in the big leagues today who get caught that way. I saw one last summer and wondered why the base runners did not take advantage of it. That is one reason why I have the belief that ball players do not study their business nowadays as we did twenty years ago.

Paterson, with Some Future Stars

• • •

After finishing my season in the Iron and Oil League in 1895, I was out at my home in Carnegie hunting, fishing and knocking around, when George Moreland came out to see me about joining the Pittsburgh club of the National League. He had been sent by President Kerr.*

This sounded big and, naturally, I was right smartly smoked up. Believe me, though, I didn't think about any more of those schemes to hold a fellow up and get $5 a month more.

At Moreland's urging I went in the city to see President Kerr. He offered me $100 a month and I signed up right then and there.

There was to be a disappointment, though; I wasn't to get in the big league as soon as I thought. They didn't think I was quite ready for the big show and wanted to farm me out to Kansas City.

That seemed the farthest place in the world to be then. I hadn't forgotten how homesick I got at Adrian, Michigan. So I refused to go.

"I'd much rather stay here at home with my dogs and go hunting than to go way out there and be lost," I told them. I simply couldn't make up my mind to do it.

Unless I went to Kansas City Mr. Kerr didn't want me. So that ended that. I went on back home and hunted and fished some more. That winter we also had a lot of fun playing pool and pitching horseshoes. You may not know it, but I'm pretty good at both.

There was a Mr. McKee who owned the Paterson (New Jer-

• • •

*William W. Kerr was owner and president of the Pittsburgh team from 1894 to 1897 and in 1899.

sey) club and who was in Pittsburgh looking for ball players. Shad Gwilliam told him and Ed Barrow, his manager and partner, about me. Barrow says that Gwilliam told him I'd be the greatest ball player in the world some day. This Mr. Barrow is now the business manager of the New York Yankees, was one time president of the Eastern and International leagues and was also manager of the Boston Red Sox when they won the world's championship.

WHAT HONUS LOOKED LIKE

Ed Barrow is a powerfully built man and, believe me, when he gets angry he can use his fists. He had a big black mustache in those days—I have a picture to prove it—and that impressed me a whole lot.

Barrow and McKee, taking Gwilliam's tip, came to see me. I liked Barrow from the start. He was one of the biggest, strongest looking men I ever saw. What he saw must have given him a good laugh.

In getting together material for this account Barrow helped. He wrote:

"When I got out there I asked about this boy, Honus Wagner. They told me he was in back of the poolroom pitching horseshoes with some other boys. I went back there and a big, gangly looking fellow came up to me saying he was Honus. He had the funniest legs I ever saw and wore a little flat derby with a feather stuck in it. The only thing I could think of was Weber and Fields.* Wagner looked less like a ball player than any fellow I ever saw. Just the same, something told me I had better get this boy. Everybody had told me he was a wonderful player."

• • •

*The popular New York comedy team of Joe Weber (1867–1942) and Lew Fields (1867–1941) began performing together on the Bowery at age eight. During their long professional career they typically appeared in beards, loud checked clothes, and low-crown derbies. They were beloved by millions and became the prototypes of future comedy teams. Fields was tall and aggressive, while Weber was short and the brunt of the jokes. They were noted for their slapstick antics, their dialect jokes, and their burlesques of popular plays. They opened and managed Weber and Fields Music Hall on Broadway (1896–1904), where they presented many of the leading stars of the time. Both went into semiretirement after 1930.

After my talk with Barrow I figured it would be much nearer home to be playing at Paterson than going way out to Kansas City.

My salary was $125 a month. The main part was that I always got it on time. I never had so much fun in my life as playing with Paterson. To me it seemed like a big vacation. When I went south training in my later years it always made me think of Paterson. We had fun and excitement all the time. I played both infield and outfield—I would play anywhere anybody suggested.

At that time my brother Al was playing up at Toronto. By the way, Al took part in a funny game that year.

Toronto and Jersey City were fighting it out for nothing in particular. Neither one was going anywhere—had no chance. There were less than fifty spectators in the stand, and the players simply went through the motions. Over in the little press box the official scorer and a few newspaper men were grinding away, getting horribly bored. Nobody seemed to be paying much attention to the game. The official scorer had not been paid and was sore, anyway.

They Stopped the Clock

Jersey made one run in an early inning, but later on it was tied, nobody seemed to care exactly when. After an hour or so, with everybody dozing, the umpire stopped the game and walked over to the press box.

"What inning is it?" he asked the official scorer.

"It's—let me see," said the O.S., yawning. "It's the thirteenth now. Jersey City had the game won 1–0 in the ninth, but it's a tie now. Toronto scored in the tenth. It's all right, though. Go ahead and play all night if you want to. If you can stand it we can."

Manager Barrow didn't let me do any pitching for his club, and he had a good reason. As I have said, I started out as a pitcher. When I went to Akron they started me in to pitch a game. I must have had a lot of stuff. Pete Lavelle, my catcher, used a piece of raw beefsteak in his glove. I didn't hit that steak much at that. In that game I hit seven batters and walked nine. One of those I hit was old Jake Shrader, later a big leaguer.

I reckon you think I lost that game. Not much! Even though I walked nine and hit seven. I struck out fifteen and came in under the wire. If my control had been up to my speed, I might have made a great pitcher.

And, if you'll excuse my wandering a little, I had another pitching experience that always amused me, even if it did annoy my old father as long as he lived. The old gentleman was not strong for baseball until I began to get noticed. Then he was an enthusiast—at home, I mean. He didn't know much about the game.

I had pitched a game for Carnegie against a near-by town and several of the fellows walked home with me. We had lost.

"Oh, that's all right," one of them said. "We'd have won that ball game if Honus had had any kind of support. They're giving you terrible support, old boy," he added, turning to me.

YOUNGEST MAN ON TEAM

My old dad, sitting on the porch, overheard this. He jumped to his feet, knocking the tobacco out of his pipe, and shook his fist at the boy.

"Don't you come around here making any remarks about my boy's support, young fellow," he yelled at my teammate. "I'll have you understand my boy has just as good a home as any boy in Carnegie."

Getting back to Paterson, there were some great ball players on that club that Barrow had got together. That was in 1896. Several of them have become great playing stars as well as managers.

Among the ones to be famous later were Bill Armour, manager of Cleveland at one time; Emmett Heidrick; George Smith, later manager of the Giants; and Charlie Bastian. To show you how the team impressed me, I can name every one of them right now:

Ed Barrow, manager; Bill Smink, catcher; Bill Armour, center field; Emmett Heidrick, left field; Jack Killackey, first base; Hans Wagner, third base; Charley Bastian, shortstop; George Smith, second base; Bill Hayward, right field; Sam McMackin, Charlie McCafferty and Dick Cogan, pitchers.

That is the club with which I really broke into baseball. I was the youngest player on the team.

The Baseball That Blew Up

• • •

Manager Barrow, I think, took a sort of fancy to me. I must have made him laugh. He knew that I could hit that baseball—sock the old onion, as they call it nowadays—and let me do a lot of things. I played in about every job, except pitch. He had heard about my pitching in Akron. He did let me pitch in an exhibition game once. I was always willing and eager to do anything. I was a big, husky boy and simply loved to play baseball.

While I was playing with Paterson they got up the first idea of playing night baseball. You see, that idea is not new at all.

Barrow and McKee made arrangements for our team to play the first night game at Wilmington, Delaware. They had the place all illuminated with big electric lights and it looked like it might be a success. When darkness came on and the crowd got there the prospect didn't look so good.

The light was too dim to see a line fly and it was impossible to make a good catch in the outfield. To hit an ordinary baseball would have been out of the question. They had made up a sort of baseball like the indoor baseballs they use now. It was even hard to see that.

The public was disappointed from the start. As the game went along they got worse and worse and gave everything the razz. The players began to take the thing as a joke.

Wilmington had a pitcher named Amole who was quite a kidder. He had been planning to get me all evening. The second time I was up he pitched the big white looking baseball at me and when I smacked into it the whole thing exploded and came near blowing up the place.

They had got a torpedo and put it inside one of those balls just to have a laugh on me. They certainly did get one. I'll never forget that thing flashing and going off like a cannon when I slammed it.

The crowd didn't get any laugh, though. Instead they got sore and made a rush on the box office to get their money back.

WHAT STALLINGS WOULDN'T GIVE

Before that McKee and Barrow and the Wilmington fellows had counted up and divided the money. I'll never forget the way those fellows scooted down the street to escape that crowd and save what little money was taken in.

That was the end of night baseball. I had almost forgotten that torpedo ball until Barrow reminded me of it while I was digging up old incidents.

Ed Barrow was a smarter baseball man than I realized then. He must have seen that I would land in the big league some day, so he set about to get a good price for me. There were scouts around there every day toward the end of the season. There were five of them on the bench at one time.

George Stallings, who was managing the Philadelphia club, came

As the owner of the Paterson, New Jersey, franchise in the Atlantic League, Ed Barrow signed Honus Wagner in 1896. Barrow is most remembered for the creation of baseball's greatest dynasty—the New York Yankees. Barrow used trades, purchases, and farm team development to build a Yankee team that would win fourteen pennants and ten World Series between 1921 and 1945. Earlier, as manager, he led the Red Sox to their 1918 World Series. Barrow was inducted into the Hall of Fame in 1953. (National Baseball Hall of Fame Library, Cooperstown, New York)

over to take a look at me. He and Barrow were close friends and Ed had tipped him off.

On that day I was playing the outfield and, in trying to show off, made two long throws to the plate. I got them entirely too long and both throws went into the grandstand, making the spectators scatter. Stallings must have been disgusted.

"Well, what will you give for him?" Barrow asked George.

"Give for him?" Stallings repeated with a sniff. "Why, I wouldn't give that big bum his carfare from here to Philadelphia."

That is why, I reckon, I did not join the Phillies. And I don't blame Stallings at that. I certainly was heaving 'em wild.

Then there came a lot more scouts. Prominent among them was Harry Pulliam, then connected with the Pittsburgh club, of which Barney Dreyfuss was the owner. Harry Pulliam, you know, was later president of the National League.

In case you do not remember that far back, Barney Dreyfuss first owned the Louisville club and when the twelve-club league was cut down to eight, he took the whole club to Pittsburgh, where he is now.

Pulliam stayed around there watching me for five days. Some days I would play good and at other times I would be bad. He decided, though, I had the makings of a ball player in me. He wanted to put in a bid.

$2,000 A GOOD PRICE THEN

Barrow, in signing me for Paterson, after Pittsburgh had signed me to be farmed out in Kansas—the scheme that didn't go through—agreed to give Mr. Kerr, president of the Pittsburgh club, first chance at my services.

Harry Pulliam finally offered $2,000 for me, which was a good price in those days. Barrow asked him to wait. He then telegraphed Mr. Kerr, who said that he also would give $2,000. That, of course, made it necessary for Barrow to sell me to Pittsburgh unless Louisville made a bigger offer.

"I'll make it $2,100," Pulliam told Barrow.

This was telegraphed to Kerr and as he never answered the message Barrow sold me to Louisville for $2,100. The funny part of it is that I went to Pittsburgh later on, after all.

There has been a good deal of talk about how I was sneaked to Louisville and all that, but the deal was made just as I have told it. Barrow kept his word. If Kerr had answered the telegram he might have got me.

Personally, I didn't care where I went. All I wanted was to play baseball, the bigger the league, the better.

In the same deal that sent me to Louisville, George Smith was sold to New York for $250. What do you know about that? George was a great ball player. He was later manager of the Giants. It was about George, I believe, that John McGraw has his first run-in with Andrew Freedman when McGraw first became manager of the Giants. The American League war was on and McGraw went out to get some players. He was particularly anxious to get Smith and signed him at a big salary, something like $5,000 or $6,000. That was a lot of money in 1901.

Just the same, Barrow sold him for $250 and New York thought they had paid a good price. For a player like that nowadays a manager would have to pay at least $50,000. They are even paying big sums like that for minor leaguers who have never been tried out in fast company.

It was at Louisville that I first met Fred Clarke and all the famous players with whom I later became acquainted. Fred, you know, was manager at Louisville before he went to Pittsburgh. What's more he was one of the greatest managers baseball has ever known.

Fred was first made manager while the team was on the road. Just to make it bad for him he pulled a bone in the very first game he played as manager. It was some play on the bases; I have forgotten exactly how it went but that doesn't matter.

Fred came back to the bench and refused to sit down, he was so sore at showing himself up before his players. He walked up and down in front of the bench and never said a word. The players kept looking around and also kept quiet. They knew their new manager had pulled a bone but they knew better than to roast the boss right off. Everything was dead quiet but everybody knew what everybody else was thinking.

Finally Fred turned to the men on the bench.

"Go on and say it," he said. "Go on. I know you think I'm a boob, so go on and tell me I'm one. Yes, I pulled a bone."

He then sat down on the bench and the gang started to laugh. They told him, all right.

By that action Clarke made himself strong with his players. He never four-flushed. After that they would tell him if he pulled one. And don't you forget that he would always tell them, too. There were no more secrets on that bench or any other bench that Fred Clarke ever managed.

Batting .375 without the
Lively Ball

● ● ●

Before leaving Paterson behind in this story it is proper, my editor tells me, to call attention to the fact that in the three years I had played professional ball I had led all the teams and all the leagues in which I had been a player in batting. Up to the time I was bought by Louisville my batting average for the three years was about .375. I guess that is why Barney Dreyfuss paid the $2,000 for me.

At Steubenville my batting average was .365, at Warren it was .369. For my first full season at Paterson the average was .354 and the second season .392. Those batting averages were considered more remarkable then than they would be now. We didn't have the lively ball then. To hit .300 was quite an event.

I am not quite sure in my mind whether it is altogether the lively ball that is causing such heavy hitting nowadays or whether

it is poor pitching. I am certain that the restrictions put on the pitcher have had something to do with it. Pitchers are not allowed to soil the ball or use any foreign substance on it, such as resin. Even the spitball is barred except in a few cases. In the old days the pitcher could go as far as he liked.

There is no doubt about the lively ball helping the batter. Some hits that shoot through the infield would have been stopped in the old days.

Right here let me bring in another subject. Much has been said about the pitchers walking Babe Ruth purposely. It has been said that they ought to give him a chance; that it is unsportsmanlike to pass him.

Everybody seems to be of the impression that the pitchers pass Ruth to keep him from getting a hit—that and nothing else. There is another thing they have overlooked: In many cases the pitchers pass Babe Ruth simply because they don't want to risk getting hit with a ball driven straight back at them. Don't forget that. Nobody was ever able to hit a ball with the tremendous force that Ruth put into a swing. It is remarkable that he has never seriously injured a pitcher. Personally I know that he is always afraid of hitting one back so hard that the pitcher can't get out of the way.

RUTH'S WALLOP A REAL RISK

If that happens he is likely to kill somebody.

Some of the players were telling me last spring about a drive Ruth hit back at Dutch Reuther. The ball struck him on the thigh and made him limp for several days. The blue spot on Reuther's leg showed the marking of the stitches of the ball.

George Herman "Babe" Ruth was baseball's first great home run hitter and the most celebrated player of his time. Beginning in 1914 as a pitcher with the Red Sox, he won 89 games in six years while setting the World Series record for consecutive scoreless innings. He converted to the outfield full-time after his sale to the Yankees in 1920, and he went on to lead New York to seven American League pennants and four World Series titles. Ruth changed the nature of the game itself, ushering in the demise of the Dead Ball Era. He finished his 22-year playing career with 714 home runs, leading the league twelve times. Ruth was inducted into the Hall of Fame in 1936. (George Brace Photo Collection)

"I'll guarantee you," declared Reuther, "he won't hit another one back at me like that."

By that he meant that he would keep the ball outside or inside so that Ruth would hit to one field or the other.

Now, if I was in the two-three hole on Ruth, I doubt very much if I would lay one over the middle and risk getting killed. Many of the pitchers have the same notion. He is passed for that reason as much as through fear of his getting a hit. That boy is a dangerous man up at the plate.

From my own observation and from talks with other old ball players, I am pretty sure that the pitching is not up to the caliber of a few years ago. The younger ball players do not seem to study their business as closely as they formerly did. It is the same with other players.

Bill Donovan, a mighty smart pitcher in his day, has the right idea.

"Whether it is a lively ball or a dead one," says Bill, "they've got to hit it, haven't they? If you let a batter get hold of one of the old balls he knocks it for a loop. It might not go as far but it would certainly go safe. The main idea is for the pitchers to keep the batter from hitting the ball on the nose. If he does that they can't beat him, even with the lively ball."

That there is a lot of truth in this is shown by the number of no-hit games pitched last season. The lively ball didn't help a bit as long as the pitcher wouldn't let them get hold of it. There were any number of shut-out games and a lot of small scores. That's when the pitching was good.

THE GREATEST HIT EVER

There is no doubt, though, that the lively ball has made a big change in base-running. Managers do not make their men steal second now except in rare cases. What's the use of trying to steal second and, maybe, getting thrown out when the next batter might come along and knock the ball out of the lot? Even if he didn't do that he has a good chance of smacking it past some infielder. In other words, there are more chances in waiting for a hit than in trying to steal second.

I have hit these lively balls. No doubt there is a difference, but, honestly, I don't believe there is as much difference as some try to make out. Just as Donovan says, the batter has to hit the ball on the nose, no matter if it is lively or dead. An India rubber ball wouldn't help a fellow who couldn't hit it.

This looks to me like a good spot to answer one of the questions that several fans have asked.

"What was the greatest hit you ever saw?" is the question.

I imagine that those who asked that question wanted to know the most remarkable hit—not necessarily the longest or hardest. I'll talk about those later.

The most remarkable hit I ever saw was made by Jack Killackey, first baseman on that old Paterson team. It was a home run, too.

The opposing pitcher laid one in the groove for Jack and with all his might Killackey hit it straight back at him like a bullet. The ball struck the pitcher in the forehead. As he fell the ball bounced off his head and landed in a box back of the first-base foul line for a home run.

There was a big row and everybody tried to argue, but there was no way out of it. That was a clean home run and the umpire allowed it.

SHORTEST KNOWN CAREER

I made a hit once that I always will remember, though it wasn't a freak.

The St. Louis club was playing the Pirates at Pittsburgh. Miller Huggins was the St. Louis manager. A fresh young pitcher had joined them and was rarin' to go. He was quite a wise boy, according to his own way of thinking—full of ideas and conversation. For several days he had been telling the other St. Louis players how he could make the so-called good hitters sidestep. He was eager for a chance to show us all up.

"How'll you pitch against Wagner?" Huggins asked him.

"There's only one way to do it," he said. "I don't see why others haven't thought of it. Why, I'll pitch three fast balls right at his head and drive that Dutchman from the plate. It he doesn't get away he'll get his head knocked off. Then I'll curve the next three and strike him out."

Now, that sounded simple enough, didn't it?

While he was doing this talking on the bench two of the St. Louis pitchers were being hammered out of the box.

"All right, here's your chance," Huggins told the fresh youngster. "Get in there and show us some of that pitching. Make sauerkraut out of that big Dutchman."

Several of the St. Louis players waved to me in mock fear, but I didn't know the joke.

We had the bases full when the youngster started and I was up. He really did pitch at my head, but I backed off a little as I swung and happened to hit the ball squarely on the nose, knocking it over the wall for a home run.

"That'll be all," Huggins yelled to him. "The scheme don't work."

In a few days Huggins released him. That boy, who was going to knock our heads off, had the unique record of having stayed in the big league just long enough to pitch one ball. And he never came back.

I've often wanted to know how his work appeared in the official records. The papers didn't print it. To tell the truth, though, I felt sorry for that kid. I like to see them come in fresh and full of pep and vinegar.

The Art of Batting

• • •

A fan, writing to ask that I discuss the art of batting, wants to know what was the secret of my success—how I managed to hit over .300 for so many consecutive years when nobody else did.

To be candid, I don't know. There was no secret about it, however. From the time I started as a boy I simply walked up and took a slam at any ball that happened to suit me. I don't believe half of them were over the plate.

And that brings up something that might be interesting. Wilbert Robinson, who had more than twenty years' experience behind the bat, told me once that he had kept pretty fair tab on the kind of balls that were hit safely.

"Sixty per cent of the balls that batters landed on," he says, "were not over the plate. A big percentage of batters will strike out on balls right over the pan and will hit those on the inside and outside right on the nose. Most of the hits are made on balls outside."

That in a way proves that I had the correct notion in swinging at the one that suited me whether it was over or not. The batter who is particular about getting the ball just right will not make many hits. He is like the youngster who failed to offer at a single ball and was called out on strikes by Bill Klem, the umpire.

He raised the dickens of a kick.

"You can't get any hits with that bat on your shoulder, young man," said the umpire.

In the last big series between New York and Pittsburgh when the Giants were fighting to clinch the pennant I saw a pinch-hitter stand up there and take a third strike. There is no excuse for a man doing that. He is sent up there to hit and it is his business to force the opportunity if he can't get it otherwise. The trouble is they'd rather use an alibi than take a chance. They sort of fear to stand the gaff—don't want it brought to an issue.

Fred Clarke had the right idea about that.

HIT 'EM ANYWAY

One day one of our players went up with men on bases and two out and took a third strike. Everybody groaned.

"That's the worst umpiring I ever saw," declared the batter, coming back to the bench. "That ball was a foot outside."

"I don't care whether it was over or not," retorted Fred. "If they are close enough to call a strike they are certainly close enough to hit at. That kind of alibi doesn't go."

In my early days I used to make up my mind that I would hit at it whether it was a strike or not. I found I got just about as many hits that way as any other.

The whole thing in hitting a baseball is your step. If you step right and time your swing with it so that everything goes with the ball at once, you will come pretty near hitting safe. It is very much the same as what they call timing in golf. No matter how well you swing or how nicely you stand at the bat, you are not going to get results unless your step into the ball is made at the exact moment. That makes you pivot with your swing. I don't know exactly how to teach

Bill Klem is generally regarded as baseball's greatest umpire, with a career spanning from 1908 to 1940. He worked a record eighteen World Series, including five straight from 1911 to 1915. Klem was stubborn but was widely respected for the dignity and professionalism he brought to the game. He always maintained, "I never called one wrong," though in later years he would place his hand over his heart and add, "from here." Klem was one of the first two umpires inducted into the Baseball Hall of Fame in 1953. (National Baseball Hall of Fame Library, Cooperstown, New York)

that to anybody, but once you get the feel of it, you'll know exactly what I mean. The golfers all know.

Then when you hit you must go right on through with the swing. That gives distance. If a batter steps ahead of his swing or swings ahead of his step, he will either foul the ball or lift it to one of the outfielders. To check the bat when you meet the ball is worst of all. That is really nothing more than a long bunt.

"That bird certainly stands nice at the bat."

I'll bet I've heard that ten thousand times, and so have you. The scouts always comment on whether a fellow has a nice position up there or not.

Personally, I don't think it makes a bit of difference how you stand at the bat. As long as you time your step and your swing, the way you stand amounts to nothing.

NOBODY EVER TAUGHT HIM

Nobody ever taught me how to stand at the bat. They used to say I crouched like a big gorilla. I don't know whether I did or not. What's more, I never did care. I didn't even think about it. I went up there to hit the ball and I hit it the best way I could.

McGraw was a good hitter and he stood up straight, chopping into the ball with a short sharp swing. Keeler also batted in that way. On the other hand, Delehanty used to take a healthy barn-door swing and he would knock the ball out of the lot. Take Heinie Groh, for instance. What would you have thought of Heinie as a hitter if you had been sent out as a scout to look him over? That peculiar way he stands, facing the pitcher with the bat held high over his head, would have queered him with any scout. Still, Groh is a corking good hitter.

The good batter is the one who bats just like Webster wrote the English language—in his own way. The main thing—the whole thing—is to be natural. If it feels better to jump up and down like a Comanche Indian, why, do it. If you don't get any hits that way you'll soon change your mind.

An important thing is never to be in a hurry. Above all, don't try to press. If you are overanxious the pitcher will get onto it in a minute. You'll have a fat chance of getting a good one to hit at!

Always look the pitcher over carefully and give him the impression that you are not worrying about the matter. It's a cinch he's worrying as much as you are.

I am often asked if I think it advisable to change the batting style of a youngster when he comes into the big league. I do not. Many a good ball player has been spoiled by making him change his style of swing or the way he grips the bat. It makes him awkward, unnatural.

THE COBB-WAGNER GRIP

As I write this I have just picked up a little pamphlet illustrating the different grips. The accompanying photograph is the one the author of the book calls the Wagner-Cobb grip. He advises against its use explaining that it is not a good style.

That's odd enough to make me smile. Cobb and myself, according to the records, led the big leagues more than any other batters. Still, the fellow might be right.

You will notice that Cobb and myself bat with our hands some distance apart, about four inches. Most other batters keep their hands together very much like golfers do. Now, that is all right for those who like it. I have tried all the other grips and never could use any of them. My hands remind me of two horses, pulling one at a time.

With the hands apart—the Cobb-Wagner style—I have better control of the bat. I can bunt or swing hard; can swing quick, medium or slow. That grip enables me to hit high, low, inside or outside—in fact, I can take a better and more natural cut at any kind of a ball.

The divided-hand grip is good for carrying out what I have said about the step and timing. Arms, shoulders and legs work as one.

Babe Ruth has an entirely different grip. He catches the bat well on the little end with both hands locked together. His grip is very much the same as that of Frank Schulte. Both are very long hitters. It must be all right for Ruth. He brings home the bacon. Still, I feel sure that those long swingers do not have as good a chance to chip at bad balls as men like Cobb and myself would have with the divided grip.

I guess there will always be a lot of argument about the different kinds of grips, the weight of bats, the swing and so on.

Wagner and Cobb compare grips before the 1909 World Series, as Davy Jones looks on. At this their first meeting, they discovered their common use of the split grip, sometimes referred to as the Cobb-Wagner grip. (Carnegie Library of Pittsburgh)

It only goes to show that the proper notion is go up there and hit the ball in the most natural way that you know how.

When a slump gets you it won't make any difference what you do. But I will take up slumps later.

The Bug Enters
Baseball—at 2 A.M.

• • •

The first big laugh I remember having after I joined the Louisville club and was established as a big leaguer was over Rube Waddell. He came in, you know, along about the time I did. I was surprised the other day to find that most fans and a lot of players did not know that Waddell did his first good work with Louisville.

I was a green, awkward kid, unused to big league ways and especially to the fine hotels. I kept my mouth shut, though, and went right along about my business. The one thing that saved me from a lot of extra joshing, I suppose, was because I could always slam the ball. For instance, I joined the club in the middle of the season of 1897 and hit .344 my very first year.

We were on an eastern trip when Waddell joined us at Washington. He was the first real bug,* as we now call them, to get a lot of publicity over his freak stunts. Up to that time the writers took baseball very seriously and wrote about it just like the financial experts talk about the stock market.

I notice there has been a lot of discussion lately as to what started the idea that left-handed pitchers are bugs. I don't pretend to speak with authority, but I am sure that the idea started

• • •

*The term "bug" was commonly used at the time Wagner wrote this autobiography to refer to a baseball fan, or more generally, an enthusiast for any sport. For example, a contemporary issue of *Baseball Magazine* referred to Rube Waddell as a "bug" for fishing, i.e., a fishing enthusiast. The term "buggy" seems to have been more often used to imply a little off-beat, crazy or daffy. From the context of these paragraphs, however, it is clear that Wagner meant the term "bug" to refer to the sometimes off-beat antics of Waddell.

George "Rube" Waddell was one of the top lefties in pitching history, but was also among the most eccentric, colorful, and even offbeat players. He had a great fastball, curveball, and pinpoint control. In 1905, Waddell captured pitching's "triple crown," with 27 wins, 287 strikeouts, and a 1.48 ERA, leading in all categories. Known for his strikeout prowess, Rube led the American League for six years straight. He ended his playing career in 1910 and was inducted into the Hall of Fame in 1946. (George Brace Photo Collection)

with Waddell. He was certainly entitled to the honor, if it be one, of putting the left-handers in that rating. I know I had never heard of left-handers being sort of cuckoo until Waddell came along and was heard about ever afterward.

Waddell arrived at the hotel about 2 o'clock in the morning. We were all in bed since 10 o'clock.

"I'm the new star left-hander," Waddell told the clerk, "and I want to report to Manager Clarke."

"Really," protested the clerk, "I don't think you had better awaken Mr. Clarke. He went to bed early and doesn't want to be disturbed."

"Makes no difference," insisted Waddell, "I was instructed to report to him and unless I do he won't know what a great pitcher he's got."

"I'm afraid he wouldn't welcome you. My orders are not to awaken him. Why, I can fix you up with a nice room and you can call on him the first thing in the morning."

CLERK TAKES NO CHANCES

"Got to see him now," insisted the Rube. "Can't wait."

"All right, his room is number 312. I won't wake him. You can do it, if you want to risk it."

So Waddell bounded up the stairs and in a minute was knocking on Clarke's door. Fred finally woke up and wanted to know what darn fool was bothering him.

"It's me, Rube Waddell, your new pitcher," the southpaw shouted through the keyhole.

"Oh, well, tell the clerk to give you a room and I'll see you the first thing in the morning."

"Not on your life," came the answer through the keyhole. "Must see you now or I'll take the first train out of this man's town."

Clarke knew that Rube was a good pitcher—didn't want to lose him. He got up, opened the door and listened to Waddell for a half hour. Rube told him what a great pitcher he was and how he was going to win the pennant for Louisville. Fred began to think he'd have to sit up all night. He was getting nervous, but Waddell wouldn't go.

"I'll tell you what you do," Clarke finally suggested. "I know the other fellows on the team will be disappointed if they don't meet you tonight. So, you go around and wake them all up and introduce yourself."

Waddell thought that a great idea. He went away and let Clarke get to sleep again. Fred got in bed chuckling over what would happen to the other players.

Two hours later—it was 4 o'clock by that time—Clarke was aroused again by another loud knock on his door.

"It's Rube Waddell, your new pitcher, cap'n."

"Well, you either get away from there and go to bed—either that or go back where you came from. I don't care how good a pitcher you are, I've got to have some sleep."

WHY ROOM 128 DIDN'T WAKE

"Yes, Mr. Clarke, but I'm afraid something has happened. I've met all the boys except the one in room 128, and I can't wake him up. I thought maybe something was wrong and you'd like to know it."

Clarke got up again and called up the clerk to find who was stopping in room 128.

It was Dummy Hoy, the deaf-mute outfielder!

I was very young and very green then. I didn't say much about it but I used to laugh every time I looked at Waddell. I never could forget that night when he waked us all up. Dummy Hoy, a great outfielder, by the way, also enjoyed it.

You may wonder how they waked him up when it was necessary to catch a train. He could hear a bell all right but not a knock on the door. He used to tell us that the vibration would wake him.

It used to be a favorite joke of ours to have the bellboys page Mr. Hoy when we got him in a strange city. After finding him they would tell him he was wanted on the telephone. The blank look on their faces when he started to chase them was funny.

Often I have wondered how it is that men with such afflictions as Dummy Hoy and Dummy Taylor, the two prominent deaf mutes of the game, should have such wonderful dispositions. They were both the best humored, smiling men you ever saw. They could take a joke and would enjoy it just as much as the others. On the other hand you would sometimes see a big, healthy fellow, who never had an affliction in his life, as grouchy as an old bear.

The thing that impressed my young and inexperienced mind in the big league was the way they traveled all the time, but never missed a game and nobody ever had an accident.

TRAVELED 400,000 MILES

I was checking it up last week and I traveled 400,000 miles from the time I joined the Louisville club in 1897 until I finally quit the game deciding to stay at home. That is about fifteen times around the world.

In all that time I never had an accident and never missed a train.

On one occasion our uniform did not arrive, but we played just the same. You should have seen our rigs. We borrowed uniforms wherever we could, but none of them matched and a lot of the players didn't even have a full outfit. I played in long pants.

While we were in that city, by the way, Chick Frazer invited Manager Clarke and myself to go to a show. As we were about to start some of the youngsters came along. A particularly fresh one asked Clarke how they'd go about seeing a show.

"Oh," said Chick Frazer, "just tell the man at the ticket window that you are a big league ball player and they'll feel honored to pass you and your friends in. All the theaters do that."

The fresh busher took it for granted that he meant it.

We went to the theater and bought our tickets. Imagine our surprise when we got in and found all the bushers sitting in a prominent box.

The man at the window had fallen for what Frazer had thought would be a good joke. And here we were paying out our good cash.

Lajoie Thrown in for
Good Measure

• • •

In telling of my sale to Louisville I was thinking so much about myself that I forgot to mention another young ball player who made history when taken out of our league into fast company.

Billy Nash of the Philadelphia club had been over to Paterson to look me over. That was when George Stallings wouldn't even pay Barrow my carfare as full purchase price to have me with the Phillies. That's how bad George didn't want me.

Nash was very anxious to get another player named Phil Gier, then playing with Fall River in a different league than Paterson. He couldn't come to terms with Fall River and was about to give up.

"There's another young player with Fall River," he was told, "who might turn out to be a pretty good ball player. Why not take him?"

"What's his name?" asked Nash, though he wasn't interested much.

"Lajoie—Napoleon Lajoie, they call him. He can hit pretty good and ought to be a good infielder when he gets a little experience."

"I don't care much about him," declared Nash. "The man I want is Gier."

It finally wound up in Nash agreeing to pay $2,500 to get Gier when the management promised to throw Lajoie in for good measure.

When the season was over Nash went up to Woonsocket to locate the boy Lajoie and sign him to a contract, even if it didn't amount to much, as he thought.

"The boy lives here," a policeman told Nash. "He drives a cab and if you'll go over to that cab stand you will probably find him."

Lajoie was up on the box looking for a fare when Nash came up. The matter was explained to him and he was ready in a minute to sign. So Nash made out

48

the paper right there and Lajoie signed the contract, using the top of his cab for a writing table. The old paper still shows the marks.

That's how Lajoie, one of the greatest ballplayers that ever lived went to the Phillies. And let me tell you that was some team of hitters; Delehanty was of the club as well as Lajoie. When those fellows lit into a pitcher it was tough going. Delehanty made four home runs in one game. I believe he could hit a ball harder than anybody I ever saw, except Babe Ruth.

TOBACCO THAT BIT

I am trying not to ramble but it seems like I can't ever get away from my days in Paterson. As I was looking up the old dope on Lajoie, I ran across a note from a fan asking me to mention some odd plays and accidents during my days.

I reckon I am the only player in the world who ever had to play first base a half-inning with my gloved hand only, because the other was locked in my hip pocket. All of us in those days carried loose chewing tobacco in our hip pockets. Many ball players do now. That is what got me in trouble.

Our Paterson team was playing Hartford and Sam McMacklin was pitching. At the beginning of the inning I walked over to first base, picked up my glove and then reached in my hip pocket for a chew. I went to pull my hand out, and in some way caught the lining and I was locked. I couldn't get my hand out to save my life.

I must have looked funny from the bench. The players say I did. I was struggling with one hand in my pocket and waving my other at McMacklin trying to tell him not to pitch. I was helpless.

Sam evidently didn't understand. He shot the ball over and the batter hit it down to Goat Fitch at shortstop. I waved and waved, but that didn't stop Fitch. He picked up the ball and whipped it over to me like a bullet.

There was but one thing to do. So holding my bare hand in my pocket I reached up with the free gloved hand and caught the ball. In the stands and on the bench they thought I was crazy.

Finally Manager Barrow discovered there was something wrong and called to the umpire to stop the game. He came over to me and seeing the difficulty led me back to the bench. Even Barrow couldn't

Napoleon "Larry " Lajoie was a second baseman who combined grace in the field with power at the bat. He batted over .300 in 16 of his 21 big league seasons, ten times batting over .350 for a lifetime average of .339. In 1901, he left the Phillies and went to the Athletics, dominating the new American League by batting .426, leading in fielding average, and capturing the Triple Crown. His .426 batting average still stands as the American League record. He was inducted into the Hall of Fame in 1937. (George Brace Photo Collection)

get my hand free and he had to cut the pocket out with a knife so I could go on with the game. The lining had wound itself around my wrist like a rope.

You can't keep a good man down.

It was about that time that I got my first injury in baseball. I was hit on the knee or got it bruised in sliding and the knee got worse and worse. It swelled up as big as your head. The doctor was called in a day or two and they found I had water on the knee.

In those days we played on the Polo Grounds in New York when the Giants were out of town. So Ed Barrow took me to a hospital in New York and had my knee tapped for the water. I was told to stay in the hospital for a week.

I couldn't stand it, though. I never got so lonesome in my whole life. I'll never forget the day I borrowed a pair of crutches and hobbled down to the ball park.

"Mr. Barrow," I pleaded, "I can't stand it up to that hospital. Take me on the trip with you, please. I'll go on my crutches. I've got to have these fellows to talk to."

It certainly was a tragedy to me. I must have had tears in my eyes.

"All right," Barrow finally agreed. "Get up your things and we'll take you."

I made the entire trip of ten days or more on crutches and never missed a game. At the end of that time I was well. If I had stayed in that hospital I don't believe I ever would have got well.

Now that jumps me right back to the Louisville club. Fred Clarke was teaching me a lot about baseball, but, gee, I had a lot to learn. He knew I could hit, but he couldn't find any place to put me when I wasn't batting. He tried me in the outfield.

But there I had a good chance to show off my arm, but sometimes I showed it off too much. Many times I started a peg to the plate, but overplayed my hand and heaved the ball in the grandstand.

Fred encouraged me all he could, but I know he was worried to know what to do with me. In those days, you know, when a fellow was signed he was supposed to play. They didn't take on young fellows and let them sit on the bench until they had absorbed some knowledge of the game.

NOWHERE TO GO

As a matter of fact I think managers in this day and time often make a mistake in keeping a young fellow on the bench too long. Often they keep him for six months and then trade him without knowing what he really can do. There have been great players who never would have been heard of if they had been judged merely by the way they carried themselves and by their actions on the bench. In the old days we either played ball and made good or we were fired out.

I didn't know it at the time, but Clarke spoke to Barrow, my old manager, about me, saying he had not yet found the right spot for me; that I was too green and awkward in the positions I had played.

"Why don't you try him at short?" Barrow suggested. "I played him there and he did pretty well."

"Might be a good idea," agreed Clarke. "I've tried everything else. Can't do any harm in trying. Yes, I believe I'll experiment."

In a few days I was placed at shortstop, and that began my real major-league career as an infielder. I realized that I would have to learn a lot and make good and I set about to learn it. I was not a natural-born shortstop. I had to train myself to be a good mechanic and I did it by watching others and then practicing their tricks. There is a whole lot to playing shortstop besides merely stopping the ball and throwing to first. No team ever won a pennant without an experienced, skilled mechanic at short. Make no mistake about that. I'll go into more details later.

Advice to Young
Ball Players

• • •

This chapter of my experience is intended mostly for young ball players or any other youngsters who would like to improve their game. It is in answer to at least fifty requests for advice as to how a youngster should act and feel when getting his first chance in the big league.

The first thing is to feel sure that you are a good ball player and never let that get out of your mind. Be aggressive always, but be careful not to be a smart aleck. A lot of youngsters lose their real chance by thinking they know too much and refusing to listen to the old-timers. I never knew a veteran ball player who would not go out of his way to help a starter if he felt that the youngster really wanted to learn. Even the players on opposing teams will stop to coach a youngster if he isn't too fresh.

Once a youngster joins a club he should be extremely care-ful to obey all the club rules. He may not think it advisable to go to bed at 10 o'clock, or to cut out lunch, but he should remember that it is the manager's theory and it might work out best.

Personally I have my own ideas about training, but so have others. I don't think I ever went to spring training when I wasn't in as good condition when I started as when I finished. To tell the truth, spring training was always a sort of lark to me. You see, I hunted and fished all winter, played basketball, indoor baseball—in fact anything to keep busy. That strenuous sort of work had me in fine shape when I reported. I always ate what I wanted and when I wanted. I even drank beer in the old days. I don't say that would be good routine for other youngsters, but it didn't hurt me.

Whenever there is a practice, a youngster should hurry to get to it. He should practice all the time. If the team is not playing he can go out and work with the ground keepers.

This young fellow Pie Traynor of the Pittsburgh club is sure to be one of the greatest ball players in the world. He can't miss because he simply thinks and loves baseball. Often I have passed the park and seen him working out there in the morning with a single companion. One day I saw him all alone in the rain throwing a ball against the grandstand and fielding it as it bounced back.

LIKE ANY OTHER BUSINESS

"Gee," he said one day, "I wonder when they are going to play another double-header?"

Most ball players look on a double-header with dread—a double day's work for no more money. That boy Traynor would play three if the boy could crowd in the time some way.

In a way baseball is just like any other business or profession. The man who loves it so well that he wants to work out the fine points is bound to succeed. Even in the winter, Traynor keeps in perfect condition and weighs himself every other day to see if he is gaining or losing.

A manager usually takes a fancy to a boy who is eager and willing to do anything he is told, even if it is an experiment. But the boy must show that he does it willingly, with the proper spirit. You can't drive a ball player into making good. It's a hundred to one that the manager knows your capabilities better than you do yourself. You may think you are a great outfielder when he will suddenly turn you into a shortstop or even a catcher. He has observed something about you that you never knew. So always do as your manager says and don't try to figure out where he's crazy.

Don't be fresh to umpires. Those fellows can do a lot of things for you if they think you are really ambitious. They can give you a lot of tips and they are eager to do so. The same thing goes for visiting players, your own teammates or the spectators. If a fan should ask you a question, answer him in a respectful and sincere manner. At the same time don't let visiting players or anybody else walk on you.

Honus Wagner used his hunting and playing basketball to keep in shape during the off-season. From 1902 on, Wagner organized and played on teams in the Pittsburgh area, even competing with some professional teams in the area. As team leader in this 1904 photo, Honus is fourth from the left, holding the ball. *(Baseball Magazine)*

While a youngster should not be fresh, he must be ready to uphold his rights. Once he shows the white feather he is gone.

Once in the field a young player should remember never to see or hear the spectators. Your whole interest should be centered on the other club, and your brains and energy should be aimed at how to defeat them.

McGraw Takes a Fall Out of the Kid

Don't forget that ball players who have earned reputations have a certain amount of dignity. Make a point of respecting that dignity as much as you can.

Patsy Donovan, the Brooklyn manager, was telling me the other day how Tommy McMillan got in bad that way at the start, and then got over it.

McMillan had read the papers where they referred to John McGraw as Muggsy. He didn't know it, and a lot of fans today don't know it, but that always cut McGraw to the core. It offended him more deeply than any of the newspaper writers knew. In fact, it was for a long time his fighting point.

But McMillan wanted to show pep, so when he crossed the field he yelled to the Giant bench, calling McGraw "Muggsy." He did this several times. Then McGraw got aboard him. What a tongue-lashing that little fellow got!

McMillan went to Manager Donovan and inquired the reason.

"McGraw is a man well along in years," Patsy told him, "and that word always offended him. Coming from a fresh youngster it's all

More than any other con-
temporary player, Honus
Wagner observed and
admired John McGraw's
style of play and sought
to learn from his antics
and tricks on the field.
McGraw's innovations
included helping to develop
the hit-and-run, the Baltimore chop, and the squeeze
play. McGraw was also an
innovative and autocratic
manager of the New York
Giants for 31 years, win-
ning ten pennants and
three World Series. He
ranks second all-time with
2,840 wins. McGraw was
elected to the Baseball Hall
of Fame in 1937. (National
Baseball Hall of Fame
Library, Cooperstown, New
York)

the worse. You'll never get anywhere doing that. Now, I want you to go right to McGraw's office in the clubhouse tomorrow and apologize, explaining that you didn't understand."

The next day young McMillan, like bearding the lion in his den, went straight to McGraw and apologized in the most manly manner. The way he did it so impressed the Giant manager that he was, from then on, one of McMillan's best friends and advisers. He used to spend time with McMillan showing him tricks about hitting and fielding.

As I have said before, a youngster should make a point of watching some good player closely and then try to copy his method whether it be infielding, batting or base running. If he can't quite get the hang of it, ask the player in question and he will always help. If you have a weakness be frank enough to tell the older players about it. With their help you can overcome it.

WORK ON YOUR WEAKNESSES

I used to have a fault of throwing too hard and often too high to first. I talked with Hughey Jennings, George Smith and others. They helped me wonderfully.

Always work on your weaknesses. The strong points will take care of themselves.

The chances are that you will not set the world afire at the start, but don't blame it on the umpires. Watch everything that goes on about the field. In the most unexpected place you will pick up some little point that will be of help to you the rest of your life.

Freshness in some youngsters is funny. In others it gets on everybody's nerves. Not many of you can be funny. That's a sort of gift.

I remember one young fellow who went to bat with Bill Klem umpiring. He called two strikes on the youngster. The boy turned around and started a big kick.

"Remember, son," Klem told him, "these plates in the big league have corners on them."

A few minutes later he called another and the boy was out.

"They may have corners," he said to Klem as he started back to the bench, "but I'll be doggoned if this ain't the first one I ever saw with a bay window in it."

How the Umpire Looks to a Player

• • •

Umpiring is a feature in baseball that has never been given as much attention as it deserved. To answer all questions on umpires in one lump, I can truthfully say that I never yet have seen an umpire who did not try to be right and give the plays as he saw them.

Oh, I've seen some pretty rough ones, make no mistake about that. But all these boys were trying.

I was once fined $25 by a new umpire when I wasn't even on the field. I had got a day off to go fishing. This young umpire had a sort of half-baked idea of what the duties of an umpire should be. The older fellows had told him that an umpire must first impress the players with his authority—show them that he was not afraid of them.

Well, this one started badly and, I might add, finished quickly. The players started riding him from the bench. To show authority, he ordered two or three of them off.

I was getting a little prominent in baseball then and this bird figured it out that he would fix himself solid by going after one of the stars, so he said later.

"That's going to cost Wagner $25," he yelled over to the Pittsburgh bench.

He never did understand why he got such a laugh. He hadn't been in the league long enough to know the players by sight. But, sure enough, he reported to the league president by telegraph that night that he had fined Wagner $25. I got back from the fishing trip and was so notified by the office. To my mind, that is the longest range punishment I ever have had. The poor follow lasted just a week.

AND HE ASKED WILSON

Personally I always have thought the umpires gave me a square deal. Players all want the close ones their way—no exceptions. At heart, though, they know that umpires do not purposely rub it into them.

I remember one time the Pittsburgh club was playing Chicago. A long fly hit toward outfielder Wilson. It struck close to the foul line and the umpire called it fair. There was a terrible row about that. We naturally said it was a foul.

We surged around the umpire, trying to make him change his decision but there was nothing doing.

"Ask Wilson," we begged. "Just ask him. He'll tell you. Leave it."

"Well, I be doggoned if I don't do it," the umpire surprised us by agreeing.

"Hey, Wilson," we yelled as the outfielder came in. "The ump says he'll leave it to you—was that ball foul or fair?"

"It was fair," declared Wilson. "Fair by a foot."

If you ever saw a gang slink back to the bench it was us. It never had occurred to us that Wilson might agree with the umpire. We thought he'd be fighting, too.

Never again did we ever ask for a player to give his honest opinion. We didn't want justice, you see. We wanted that ball called foul, to him.

Everybody is against the umpire. Fans and players ride him when he makes a decision against us. If he makes a close one in our favor we figure it was coming to us because he made a bad one against us last year.

I have noticed that some umpires seem to give decisions in favor of the home club. Then I have seen others who appeared to always give the close ones to the visitors. But taking it all in all, my experience has shown that the decisions about break even in the long run. An umpire cannot please everybody, so if he figures it out and pleases himself he knows he has done the right thing.

What the Umpire Has to Do

A good umpire must be fearless, confident and have good judgment. He must follow the ball closely and place himself at the best angle to see the play. The most important quality, though, is to be a good judge of human nature. He must not see or hear a lot of little things that go on around him. After a little experience he knows the difference between natural kicks due to impulse and those that are deliberately intended to show him up. No umpire will ever stand being shown up. That's why they will throw you out of a game for tossing up your glove and will not bother you for calling them names.

A good umpire forgets that a crowd is present. The whole affair is between him and the players. The minute anybody tries to get the crowd in—well, that fellow is in bad with the umpires. He should be.

An umpire has a lot of work to do. He must keep the game moving rapidly so as to please the crowd. He is what you might call a stage manager. It is up to him to stage the show badly or enjoyably. In addition, an umpire must know the rules from A to Z and must be so familiar with their application that he can make a decision on the instant and be right. A big majority of players do not know the real fine points of the rules. A whole lot of them have never read the rule book in their lives.

It has just struck me that it might be a good idea to select an all-American team of umpires, just as we do ball players. Later on I'm going to name the best ones during my time and explain why.

But to answer an inquiry—the worst decision I ever saw was made by Umpire Byron, and he made it on me.

Pittsburgh and New York were playing at Pittsburgh. I was stealing third and the catcher threw the ball into my feet, making it impossible for Devlin—I think it was Devlin—to pick it up. We both got in a tangle as I slid through a cloud of dust. The ball was bound under my arm where nobody could find it. With the ball still caught under my arm I started for the plate while the New York infield was looking for it. No one seemed to know what had become of it. About ten feet from home the ball dropped on the base line.

McGraw Puts One Over

Now here's where McGraw got in his fine work. He rushed up to Umpire Byron, who had run down to third base to make the decision, and told him I had carried the ball to the bench in my hand.

"If you don't believe it, go to the bench and make them give it to you," he urged Byron.

About this time McGraw's attention was called to the ball lying in the base path. Up to that time his back had been turned.

"That proves it," he said to Byron. "See. Wagner just rolled it out."

Byron knew that something unusual had happened. He scratched his head, not knowing what to do.

"You're out!" he finally called out to me, "for carrying the ball to the bench in your hand."

Well, you can imagine the new row that started. We milled all over the place. But Byron stuck to his decision.

The game went into extra innings and we lost.

Pittsburgh protested the game but the president of the league decided against us on Byron's written statement that I had carried the ball to the bench in my hand and rolled it out again.

I never did get over that decision, it was so unfair. The umpire, you see, never did ask me where the ball had come from. He simply took McGraw's word for it because he didn't know what else to do. McGraw started the argument as a bluff and went through with it. He always thought it a good joke. That's where he won by outtalking me.

An All-American
Selection of Umpires

• • •

For my all-American selection of umpires I have decided that five would be the right number. I have selected them from all I saw during my thirty or more years in professional baseball. Here they are:

Billy Evans, Bob Emslie, Hank O'Day, Bill Klem, Cy Rigler.

That would be most too many for a world's series. In fact I had intended to pick out four, but the more I figured the more I made up my mind that it would be unfair to leave out a single one of those.

I've heard of umpires selecting the best ball players, but this is the first time I've heard of a ball player selecting umpires. It only goes to show that we all get a little mellow when our hair gets gray and we think about things. I don't believe there is one of those umpires who ever made a decision in his life that he didn't think exactly right.

Hank O'Day and Bill Klem, for instance, don't believe there were ever any close decisions. "They're either out or they ain't," says O'Day.

"Say Bill," I asked of Klem one night when we were talking as friends, "how do you feel after you've made a bad decision and what do you figure on doing to square it?"

"I don't know, Honus," he said—and he meant it. "I never made one."

I have put Billy Evans at the top, not because he was necessarily superior to the others, but because he was born with a perfect disposition for the umpiring business.

Evans never got into an argument with a player. He had a way of listening that would make the player think he was giving deep consideration to what he said. Then he would make his decision just like a judge does after listening to the testimony. And, remarkably enough, the player would take it that way.

I don't believe that Evans was ever a professional player, but he certainly knows exactly how a ball player thinks. He has a wonderful knowledge of the game—its history, the rules and everything. He has the same kind of knowledge about other sports. Billy has rare judgment in critical moments and knows exactly how to handle a game to please the public. He never gets riled at what he hears about—pretends not to have heard it. Only a good judge of human nature could do that.

Evans is particularly good on balls and strikes and is the best in the business on fair and foul balls. I don't believe he ever made a mistake on fair and foul balls. He knows all the tricks of the players so well that it is impossible to fool him. A player could always reason with him, but he would not and will not stand for bulldozing. Evans will admit mistakes if you show him where he is wrong. He has the absolute confidence of players and public.

Bob Emslie I regard as the greatest of all the umpires on base decisions. Some kind of instinct seemed to guide him on all close plays. If a man was stealing second and I missed touching him by a quarter of an inch, Emslie would see it. He knew baseball, of course. His strong point, though, was his fine judgment on plays not covered by the rule book. Bob was and is a quick thinker. He saved many a bad situation by making a quick decision on some point not covered by the rules. Nine times out of ten the players would feel satisfied that he had done right.

At one time the players tried to say that Bob had poor eyesight. Some New York player offered to bet him that if an apple and an orange were put on second base he couldn't tell which was which from the plate. That fall Emslie went out and won the trap-shooting tournament in the Middle West. After that the apple and orange bet was forgotten.

Hank O'Day always was a wonderful all-round umpire. He was good on balls and strikes, on the bases and on fair and foul balls. O'Day's long suit was in making difficult decisions. If the play was very difficult he would think it over for a moment and then make his ruling. Ninety-nine times out of 100 he was correct.

At the age of 22, Billy Evans was the youngest man ever to become a Major League umpire. He was known for his fairness and integrity over a 22-year career. After he retired from umpiring, he became the general manager of the Cleveland Indians (1927–35) and the Detroit Tigers (1947–51). Evans was also a writer of many articles, including a syndicated column from 1920 to 1927, and a book, *Umpiring from the Inside.* He was elected to the Baseball Hall of Fame in 1973, the third umpire ever selected. (National Baseball Hall of Fame Library, Cooperstown, New York)

Most players never stop to think how good an average an umpire must have. A player has to look over not more than twenty balls or strikes in a game. The umpire has to decide on more than 100. The player can make two mistakes out of four and get away with it. The umpire is in trouble if he makes one out of 100.

Cy Rigler was a much better umpire than he ever got credit for. He was a good all-around man with a lot of nerve and rare judgment. There was a bird you couldn't bulldoze! At the same time he would hear what you had to say. A player could talk to Cy without being afraid.

Rigler was a rare judge of ball players. In his winter months he acted as scout for a while, until a rule was made to prevent umpires from doing that. By the way, I often have wondered why more old umpires are not turned into scouts. They have an opportunity to see all kinds of players and to know just what is required in a good man. Their observations on pitchers often have been quite a help to managers.

Bill Klem I have saved for the last, not because he stands fifth in ability, but because I wanted to talk about him. Bill has given me many a laugh, and many a sore spot, too. He is a wonderful umpire, don't ever forget that. I doubt if there was ever a better man than Bill Klem. He is great on decisions that require sure judgment in very important moments. Klem is an ideal umpire to handle any unusual or important series of games. He takes his business very seriously and has a deep pride in turning out a good job. Klem is fearless and never made a mistake. He claims there are no close plays.

Bill is so good in every department that it is hard to pick his really strong point. I guess though, he stands above them all in making decisions on plays at the home plate.

Klem has the players' confidence and knows all their tricks. He, too, will reverse his decision if anybody can show him he's wrong.

"You're a great ball player, at that," said Klem as Clarke passed.

"And you're a great umpire," Fred retorted. "I'd say you are a model umpire."

Klem swelled up for a moment and then turned.

"You know what a model umpire is?" Clarke asked. "Look in the dictionary tonight."

The next afternoon Clarke was on the third base coaching line. He made some slight remark.

"Get out of the game," Bill roared at him. "I am a model umpire, am I. I'll show you how model I am. Get out of the park!"

That night we stole Klem's dictionary and he had the definition of a model umpire marked.

It said: "Model—A small imitation of the real thing."

The Pitcher I Found It Hardest to Hit

• • •

The pitcher I found the hardest to hit in all my years of baseball was Jack Taylor of the Chicago Cubs.

That is an answer to a dozen questions I have received and I feel sure it will be a surprise. Most of the writers who have been kind enough to suggest these subjects and who inquired about the toughest invariably asked if he were Mathewson, Alexander, Cy Young, Mordecai Brown and so on. Not one thought of Jack Taylor.

Just the same I had more difficulty in getting safe hits off Taylor than any other man I ever faced. He was not a wonderful pitcher, at that. He did not have anything like the stuff of these I have mentioned. Somehow, though, I simply couldn't do a thing with him. I would size up the ball exactly and know just what was coming but it didn't get me anything.

One season I went for two months or more without getting a single hit off Taylor. I hit many of them squarely on the nose and got line drives all right, but they would go straight into the hands of some outfielder. A thing like that gets a hitter's goat.

In one game at Pittsburgh I had been up twice without touching Taylor. The players on our club had begun to kid me about it.

"Hey, Honus," Claude Ritchey called to me in a joke, "maybe his weakness is left-handed hitting. Why don't you turn around?"

This got a good laugh from the players as I had never batted left-handed in my life. Never could swing a bat well that way.

"That might be a good idea," I said to myself, walking up to the plate.

Being thoroughly disgusted and taking the whole thing as a joke, I walked up there and took the opposite side of the plate.

There was a murmur of surprise from the fans. Even the umpire looked as if he thought me crazy.

"You know where you are standing?" he asked.

Just then Taylor laid one over and I punched at the ball with my awkward left-handed swing—swung the bat like a woman.

HIS LEFT-HANDED SWAT

I'll be doggoned if I didn't hit that ball right on the nose and whipped it down the right foul line for two bases. Everybody, including the players, roared with laughter. Taylor called me a lot of names.

But that had turned the tide. For the rest of the season I hit as well off Taylor as the rest of the pitchers. And I never did bat left-handed again, either.

A batting slump is the most puzzling thing in all baseball. It hits every batter at some time or other and once the blight falls on a fel-

John W. "Jack" Taylor was an award-winning right-handed pitcher for the Chicago Cubs, beginning in 1898. His 10-year career average ERA was a low 2.66. Wagner identifies Taylor as the pitcher most difficult for him to hit. Wagner once faced Taylor left-handed after two months of going hitless against him. (George Brace Photo Collection)

low he has no mental rest until it is over. Nothing he tries seems to go right. As a result he gets to pressing, trying to kill the ball. That naturally makes him worse.

There is no explanation of how a batter will get that. Personally, I think it a matter of the mind more than the eye and the muscles.

It might interest you to know that a majority of the ball players who received my request to submit suggestions for subjects in this autobiography asked for an explanation of the batting slump and how to get over it.

In the first place I believe a batter, after failing two or three times in succession, gets overanxious. In my case I found it all in the step. I would either take too long a step into the ball, too short, too late, too quick, too slow, too straight and a tendency to pull away. As a result I tried to hit everything and never could get the pitcher in the hole. Then I found myself unable to wait and became hopelessly confused.

This, in a way, applies to driving in golf. Lots of them tell me they get in slumps like that. It also applies to everyday business and to life in general. Once a fellow gets mixed up, goes off his routine, he starts plunging around and is completely off balance.

My suggestion for a way to get out of the batting slump is the one everybody tells you, but you cannot do—forget it. That is easier said than done. How can a man forget a thing that is the only thing in his mind?

START ALL OVER AGAIN

As I have just said, I overcame my batting slump against Taylor by batting left-handed. That might help others. The main thing, though, is to look yourself over and start right from the bottom, as if you were learning all over. Bat in a careless way, as if you didn't give a hang what happened.

A batter should start in by taking a short step and an easy swing, as if he simply wanted to tap the ball. Time the ball and don't be overanxious to hit. Wait the pitcher out as long as you can. If you get two or three balls then make up your mind to hit the first good one. Don't worry about a hit.

A batter in a slump should take an unusual lot of batting practice and bat as if he were experimenting. Above all things don't blame the bat. I have known many hitters to throw away their bats while in a slump and buy new ones. Golfers who go wrong in their drives often throw away their drivers and buy new clubs. As a result they are worse off than ever. It is never the fault of the bat.

For expert batters—big leaguers—it is a good idea in getting out of a slump to simply hit the ball on the nose. They should never try to place it.

In my whole experience the most satisfactory batting I ever accomplished was while coming out of one of these slumps.

In 1899 while playing with Louisville, we had been losing regularly. I could not hit the ball and the other heavy batters were in the same fix. The fans had started to ride. That, by the way, is the worst part of the batting slump. It is a sure tip-off as to how bad you look. The players notice it long before the fans.

On the day of this particular game we were playing Pittsburgh and the fans knew that I came from there, that the Pittsburgh section was my home.

In the very first inning they gave me an extra hard razzing. Some loud-mouthed ones were begging the Pittsburgh club to take me home with them; that they were tired of looking at that Dutchman.

Tannehill pitched for Pittsburgh and he was a corking good pitcher. Just the same I rose out of my slump and slammed him for a home run the first time up. Later I got another home run. Before the day was over I had four hits. My second home run, which came in the ninth inning, won the game for us by a score of 2 to 1. My home runs were the only scores Louisville made.

In all my time I think that gave me more satisfaction than any batting stunt I ever did. The fans did not try to wish me on Pittsburgh after that. None of us realized then that in a short time I would actually be in Pittsburgh playing on the home team. They never dreamed that Louisville would be out of the league forever and that the whole team would be moved to Pittsburgh. Still, that is what happened.

There seems to be some misunderstanding among a few modern-day fans as to how I went to Pittsburgh. I was never traded there or sold.

When I got in the National League it was made up of twelve clubs. This proved a failure. The circuit was entirely too big.

I didn't know much about baseball politics in those days—didn't care—but there was a lot of hollering from Baltimore and Louisville about being dropped out. It was particularly loud from Baltimore where they had the greatest ball club of that time. Still, the Baltimore team, with all its status, didn't pay.

So the league was cut down to eight clubs. Barney Dreyfuss got the Pittsburgh franchise and the whole Louisville team was moved over there. Some of the Pittsburgh players stayed, but not many. I only know I was tickled to death to be shifted over with a chance of being with my own friends for the rest of my playing days.

The Test of a Star Team

• • •

Having been asked to give an opinion as to what department of baseball comes nearer showing the difference between a star ball club and an ordinary one, my answer is: The running and stealing of bases.

There is quite a difference between running bases and stealing bases. It is a different art. Among ball players, to run the bases means to get every possible advantage out of a hit. To steal bases means to get every possible advantage on the base paths without a hit.

I notice that fans and even expert writers often make the mistake of referring to a player as a great base runner when they really mean a great base stealer. There are many marvelous base runners who rarely ever steal a base. On the other hand, there are some men who seem to have a gift for stealing bases, but who often fall down in running out their hits.

To my mind, the art of base stealing has declined a whole lot in the last few years, due mostly to the lively ball. Managers, figuring the percentage of chances, seem to have decided that there is less chance in trying for a steal than in waiting for the batter to get a hit. With the lively ball he has more chances of knocking a grounder through the infield than formerly. That makes the hit-and-run the outstanding play, because it gives the runner a double chance. If the batter fails to hit, the runner may have the base stolen anyway. If the ball is hit through the infielder the runner takes an extra base. That is why most smart managers use it ahead of all other plays.

The oddest and most amusing—to the spectators—base-running stunt I ever saw happened with the Pirates in a game in Chicago. It was not funny to me.

It was the beginning of the ninth inning, and the Cubs had us 4 to 3. Suddenly there came a break. The first man got on. Then came a couple of lucky breaks in the infield and we got the bases full with none out. I was next at bat. This looked like a cinch. A hit, a fly ball—anything—would score one run and tie the score. A hit or two would break up the game.

THEY FALL WITHOUT A BLOW

I never felt surer of winning a ball game in my life. As I stood there I would have bet a thousand to one that we would win.

Kling was catching. And, by the way, there was a great catcher. The whole Chicago infield suddenly went into a conference. Kling ran out to the pitcher and after a lot of nodding of heads he came back behind the bat. Taylor was pitching.

I crowded on to the plate, but the pitch was far out to one side.

John Kling was a catcher in Major League baseball from 1900 to 1913, playing for the Chicago Cubs, the Boston Rustlers & Braves, and the Cincinnati Reds. Kling was an exceptional defensive catcher and also had a decent bat. He was with the Cubs when they won four National League pennants and two World Series titles between 1906 and 1910. In his career of 1,260 games, he batted .271 with 20 home runs and 513 RBIs all-time. He had 1,151 hits in 4,241 at bats. (George Brace Photo Collection)

In a flash, Kling, who had figured the situation out right, whipped the ball down to second and the runner, who had taken a big lead, was caught flat-footed. Seeing he couldn't get back to second the runner started for third. At the same moment the runner on third started for home.

The Cubs then switched the play and caught the third-base runner in a chase between third and home. He finally slid back to third safely, and the play shifted again, the second-base runner being caught going back to second again. This kept up for fully five minutes. Again the man was caught off third. By this time every man on both clubs, including the substitutes, was out on the lines, telling the runners what to do. The spectators were also shouting advice. I was simply standing there with the bat in my hand.

They ran those players up and down the lines for fully ten minutes, with everybody confused, the whole game in a jam.

Finally they nailed the man at the plate when Kling turned and again caught the runner between third and second. After a long chase they ran him down. Just as he slid into second to be touched out the Cubs looked up, and there was the other runner tearing down from first to second. In time they got him.

All this time the crowd didn't know what was going on. Neither did we, for that matter. All was confusion. Finally Umpire O'Day walked up to the plate.

"They're all out!" he yelled, waving his arms to include the whole diamond.

Then for the first time we realized that three men were out.

In other words, I walked up to the bat with the bases full and none out. On one pitched ball the entire side was put out and I was left standing there. Not a ball had been hit.

I don't believe such a play was ever duplicated in all baseball.

You can well imagine how we sat and looked at each other as we rode back to the hotel.

GET THE LEAD IN STEALING

The art of base-stealing and base-running does not necessarily rely on speed. The main thing in stealing a base is to get the lead. Without a lead a runner is merely wasting his time, no matter how fast he is. The important thing is to study the pitcher closely and find out just what kind of a move he makes in throwing to first base and to the plate. Nearly every one of them has some little mannerism that is noticeable to a close student.

Louis Drucke of the Giants had a fault of lifting his right heel off the ground just before he turned to throw to first. If he didn't do that we knew he would throw to the plate. That gave us a chance to take a lead. Drucke had great luck in beating our club in the old days, notwithstanding this weakness. It took McGraw a long time to discover how we knew when to take a lead, but he finally got it. Then he made Drucke change his habits. That is an illustration of how close a young pitcher has to be watched.

Fans often think a pitcher is wonderful, but they do not know of these little faults. Until they are corrected the pitcher is not properly seasoned for fine work.

After a runner thinks he has outguessed the pitcher he gets his lead and starts. Mind you a base-runner knows that the pitcher is also studying him to see what move he makes for a bluff or a real start. Therefore, the runner must watch himself as well as the pitcher. He must stand exactly the same when he intends to bluff or to start. His move is to baseball what a good poker player's face is to poker. He must never tip his mitt.

Once a man starts he must go through. That thing of trying to get back to the base if caught is foolish. There is more chance of going through with it. No man can be a good base-runner without a good hook slide, and he must be able to slide either to the right or to the left. The direction in which to slide can nearly always be determined by the motion of the infielder who starts to cover the bag.

GO THROUGH WITH IT

Let me advise a young ball player: If you start a slide go right on through with it, whether you are caught or not. If you attempt to check your slide you are likely to break a leg. Don't forget that the pitcher is as worried as you are. The main idea is to make him do the worrying.

Ty Cobb has the right theory in base-running. He always took the chances and tested the other fellow's nerve instead of letting the

Many regard Ty Cobb as the greatest baseball player of all time. His batting accomplishments are legendary—a lifetime average of .367, 4,191 hits, 12 batting titles (including nine in a row), 23 straight seasons hitting over .300, with three seasons over .400, and 2,246 runs. Cobb stole 892 bases during a 24-year career with the Detroit Tigers, and later the Philadelphia Athletics. When he retired in 1928, he was the holder of 90 Major League records and he received the most votes of the first five players elected to the Baseball Hall of Fame in 1936. (George Brace Photo Collection)

opposition test his. There is a lot in that. Make them do the worrying. That is true in any business. Instead of letting the other man keep you worried as to what he is going to do, you should take the offensive and make the defense worry as to what you are going to do.

Cobb, for instance, was never worried about being cut by the baseman's spikes. But they were always worried about being cut by his. There is just as much danger one way as the other, but his aggressive and determined manner made them feel on the defensive always. I don't believe that Cobb or any other good base-runner ever deliberately cut into a baseman. No ball player wants to hurt another. The good ones, though, always want to win. That is all they think of.

The Plays That Take Baseball Genius

• • •

I am often undecided as to which is the most interesting in baseball—the studying of opposing pitchers and infielders so as to steal a base or their perfecting of a defense to prevent base-stealing.

Skill in offsetting the fast base running of an opposing team marks the difference between a really great infielder and just a plain infielder who can pick up grounders and throw the ball.

I wrote some time back that no pennant was ever won with an inexperienced shortstop or second baseman. It simply can't be done. To work perfectly around the bag, each of those men must be a skilled mechanic so drilled in the tricks of his trade that they become second nature. I have also said that a base-runner must watch the pitcher and the infielders closely so as to learn what their various moves mean. He must remember, though, that they are also watching him.

Fans often ask me how it is that an infielder can make a great stop and throw to the right base without having any time whatever to study out the situation. Now, some players do that by instinct, but not many. Most of them do it by preparing their plans in advance.

Every good infielder or outfielder on a team figures that the ball will be hit to him. He sees the situation on the bases and decides just where he will throw the ball in case he does get it. Therefore, he doesn't have to figure. He gets the ball and whips it to the spot already decided on in advance.

If the bases are full, with none or one out, for instance, every infielder knows that he must throw the ball to the plate. He doesn't have to hesitate. If there is a man on first base and a grounder is hit to the infield, the infielder knows that he must get the ball to second base for a double play or a force-out. To prepare for this the second baseman indicates to the shortstop, or the other way around, which is to cover the bag. If the batter hits left-handed there is usually no need to give a signal. The shortstop will cover unless, by chance, he gets the ball.

CROWD MISSES FINE POINTS

It is easier, you know, for the shortstop to make a play on a base-stealer than for the second baseman to do it. That is why he does the most covering as a rule. The second baseman is often between the runner and the bag, which makes it more difficult for him. Still, if the batter is a hard left-field hitter, the second baseman signals that he will cover. In this case the shortstop might leave his position only to have the batter hit right through the hole.

There are many ball players who are specialists—expert on certain plays. Oddly enough the crowd or the writing experts seldom know this.

One of the most difficult plays to make in all baseball is the shortstop or second baseman taking a low throw from the catcher—one that hits them in the feet—as the runner is stealing. The fellows tell me I was good at that on account of my big hands, but I think Joe Tinker was about as clever at that as any ballplayer that ever lived. Another great man on that particular play was Arthur Fletcher. Miller Huggins, the present manager of the New York Yankees, was a bearcat in taking low throws. This is remarkable in his case because of his small size and correspondingly small hands. Huggins had no fear of the base runner, and that also helped.

The other wonderful players on that low-throw play were Claude Ritchey of the old Pirates, Eddie Collins of the White Sox, and Harry Steinfeldt of the old Cubs.

Another of the most difficult plays in all baseball is handling a sacrifice bunt when first and third bases are occupied and none out. The infield is guessing from the moment it starts. If either the first baseman or the third baseman tries to cover his base it is almost impossible to beat the play. To overcome this we doped out a scheme in the old days where the third baseman would go in for the bunt and the shortstop would cover, provided, of course, the ball was bunted toward third, as it should be.

The best man I ever saw on that play was Tommy Leach, third baseman of the old Pirates. Jimmy Collins was also great at it.

The play at first base is broken up by the first baseman coming in and the second baseman covering. That is not nearly so difficult, though it seems like the same play. The second baseman is accustomed to covering first base more than the shortstop is third. Besides, one of them must be ready to cover second if necessary.

Hal Chase, I believe, was the originator of the play where the first baseman gets a bunt and throws to third when there is a runner on second. That takes great speed. I have seen other players do it, though.

While on the subject of hard plays to make, don't forget that of making shoestring catches on liners hit to the outfield. To do that a player must have great nerve and also accuracy. If the ball gets by him it may go for three bases or a home-run. Often it is better to play it safe and take the ball on the bounce. The greatest men on making those low shoestring catches I ever saw were Jimmy Slagle, Jimmy Sheckard and Dummy Hoy.

Another standing problem for infields is stopping the double steal with runners on first and third bases. The best men I ever saw at that were pitchers Christy Mathewson and Joe McGinnity. There are several defensive plays but they had the best. Their scheme was for the catcher to throw a foot over their head, and throw hard, as if the ball was going all the way to second. The catcher can't be timid about it. If he does the base runners will get on. Now, just as the ball goes over the pitcher's head he intercepts it. Immediately he turns toward second base. As he makes a right turn the pitcher gets a view of third base. If the runner has started off third the pitcher tosses the ball to that base and catches him flat-footed. If the man on third holds the bag the pitcher goes right on through with his turn and nails the man going to second. Then if the man on third takes a late start for home, the second baseman or shortstop has plenty of time to get him at the plate, the play having held him up.

He Didn't Touch Home

To make that play requires the quickest kind of thinking and the quickest kind of action. Also the pitcher must have a sure pair of hands and never drop the ball.

Of course, it would be impossible for a left-handed pitcher to make this play with the same ease. It is an awkward turn for him.

When the bases are full and there are not two out every man on the infield knows exactly what to do in advance. He throws to the plate. The catcher then throws to first and makes a double play. That is a copper-plate play. No other plan is ever used. As the catcher does not have to touch the runner there is plenty of time.

Even that play, though, goes wrong sometimes. We were playing Cincinnati at Pittsburgh once and had the bases full with none out. Larry McLean was catching for the Reds. The next batter hit a grounder to the second baseman, who made a perfect throw to the plate. Larry, after catching the ball, turned and threw to first, getting the batter. But our man on third came on in and scored. McLean had found the play so easy that he stood in the catcher's box to make the throw to first and forgot to touch the plate

Some Tips for
Amateur Teams

• • •

As this appears, colleges all over the country will have begun their preliminary work toward turning out good ball teams. Some of the colleges have provided themselves with experienced professional coaches, but most of them have not.

College baseball is quite different from that of the major leagues because the professional teams can buy men to fill certain gaps. If the position is weak they can get a capable man to fill it. At any rate, they have a chance of doing it by trade or purchase. The colleges cannot do that. They must get the best out of what they have.

The colleges, for instance, may have an excellent fielding shortstop who cannot hit. Or they might have a good hitter who is a poor infielder. It is sometimes impossible to get a combination of both.

As a rule the college players do not hit well. I guess that is because hitters are scarcer than good fielders and throwers. In the minor leagues, even, there are any number of marvelous fielders and throwers who cannot make the big leagues simply because they are weak hitters.

While I was playing with Pittsburgh I was employed as coach at Carnegie Tech. I found the college boys eager to learn and willing to attempt anything that I suggested. It was evident, though, and naturally so, that they did not appreciate the finer points of the game. Even if they did, they did not have the skill to execute plays that would be everyday affairs for the majors.

It therefore occurred to me to teach them fundamentals. I prepared regular examination papers for the boys to study. It was of great help. They forget so many little things in putting together a team.

In the hope that it may help some college which is unable to engage a big-league coach, I want to present the first block of five questions that I gave my class at Carnegie Tech. The answers to these questions are apparent in most cases, but they are good points to remember. Some of them are open to discussion. By the discussion of them I think the college players will arrive at many good conclusions. They are intended as a defense against straightaway hitting.

FIVE POINTS FOR AMATEURS

Now, look these over:

1. Do you use a signal on the defense to let your infielders and outfielders know what kind of a ball is to be delivered to the batter?
2. Do you intentionally pass a dangerous batter when men are in scoring positions?
3. Do you depend on the pitcher to field as many ground balls as possible, and not depend entirely upon the infielders?
4. Does your catcher always give the sign for the kind of ball to be delivered?
5. Do you have your catcher backing up first on an infield ball with no outs?

Those five questions I think worthy of study. If the amateur coach and the amateur captain will see that the men keep those things in mind, it will make a great difference in defensive play. I would not give more questions at one time. Too many would tend to confuse rather than help. Later I will present some others.

The use of a signal to let infielders and outfielders know what kind of a ball is to be pitched is very essential. It gives them a definite cue as to where to place themselves for batted balls. Also it lets the shortstop or second baseman know who will cover second after a man gets on first.

If, for instance, a ball is curved in to a left-handed batter the chances are nine out of ten that he will pull it between first and second or into right field. If this is known in advance the second baseman and right fielder both can shift so as to get in front of the ball.

An expert outfielder like Tris Speaker can tell almost exactly where a certain batter will ordinarily hit a certain kind of pitch.

On the other hand, if the pitcher intends to pitch a fastball outside the plate to a left-handed batter, he will cut it toward left field. It is very difficult for a batter to get hold of that kind of a ball, especially an amateur.

The shortstop and second baseman are always in position to see what kind of sign the catcher gives the pitcher. One of them should tip off the others. In case of doubt the catcher can often move the outfield around by merely waving his hand.

THINK OF THE NEXT BATTER

As to passing a batter in a pinch, it depends entirely upon how dangerous he is. The next batter also has to be considered. It is never advisable to put a man on base who might bring in the winning run unless the succeeding batter is the weakest man on the club. Those chances have to be weighed. Remember that the chances are always against any batter getting a hit. If, for example, he is a .300 hitter, the chances are that he will get a safe hit one time in three. But if there is a man on third ready to score on a long fly, that is not necessary.

As to the third question, certainly the pitcher should do as much fielding as possible. A pitcher who can hold his position perfectly is often more valuable to a team than the star who cannot field a ball.

The answers to the others are rather obvious. It is well to keep those pointers in mind, though—to be sure that they are not forgotten in the heat of the game. The amateur, above all things, must learn to keep himself from getting excited.

A common fault among amateur outfielders is the running down and catching of long fouls when there is a man on third and not two out. In their eagerness to make a good showing, the outfielders forget that if the ball is caught the runner will score. It is hard to let it go, but they must keep their heads and do so. Some of our best major league outfielders make that mistake sometimes. I have seen important games lost by it.

I know that some of the old-timers will laugh at these simple suggestions. But they should remember that these boys are not playing ball for a living and that they are liable to be carried away in the excitement of their game. All of us had to learn our first reader at some time. At any rate, we have to remember what we did learn.

All the Way to Clubhouse

To show you that a ball player often forgets, there have been two or three instances in baseball where an outfielder ran to the clubhouse after making a catch with men on bases, thinking that there were two out.

In one game at the Polo Grounds in New York an outfielder—Ball, I think it was—caught a long fly when the bases were full and one out.

Something got crossed in his bean and he started straight for the clubhouse. The players started chasing him, trying to tell him that there were not two out. He, thinking they were chasing him to get the ball, waved his hand gaily and dashed through the exit gate leading to the clubhouse. They finally chased him right up into the locker room and had to wrestle him down to get the ball. In the meantime all three runners had scored.

Even as clever an outfielder as Red Murray once did a similar trick. He caught a ball with one out and started away with it, allowing a man to score. They caught Murray, though, before he could get out of the park.

I was playing in a game against Cincinnati once and was on first base. The pitcher and catcher seemed to have a misunderstanding as to what to pitch. While the pitcher was peering at the catcher's glove and shaking his head, I deliberately walked down to second base—didn't even run. In his worry over the signal he had forgotten all about a runner being on first.

I really feel that I wouldn't be doing any good for myself or for baseball if I didn't try to help out the college and other amateur players. As I go along I will give them some more little points to think over.

Do You Know a Bonehead when You See One?

• • •

The most misused word in all baseball, to my way of thinking, is bonehead. Anytime I hear some spectator yell "Bone!" or "Bonehead!" at a player, I always turn to look. Eight times out of ten the man who used the expression is the bone himself. It is quite common among fans to call any play they do not understand a bone. It sort of sounds smart to them, I reckon.

People are queer things, at that. Why is it, I've often asked myself, that some spectators take more joy out of seeing somebody pull what they call a bone than they do at seeing him make a wonderful play?

Of course, there have been some very funny bone plays in baseball, plays that are just as funny to the players as to the fans. At other times though, players make a really wonderful play only to have it labeled a bone simply because the fans do not understand baseball well enough to get the point.

To give you a case in point:

Heinie Wagner, at one time a star with the Boston Red Sox, was terribly berated one day for pulling a bone when, as a matter of fact, he had pulled one of the smartest plays I ever heard of.

Heinie was on second with one out when he got the signal for the hit-and-run play. With the swing of the pitcher's arm he started for third. The batter hit the ball all right, but Heinie could see it was a soft liner going straight into the shortstop's hands. If it was caught, Heinie would be doubled up at second.

So Heinie stood still and let the ball hit him.

"Oh, you bone—you bonehead!" yelled the fans.

Charles "Heinie" Wagner, Honus's namesake, broke into the big leagues in 1902 as a 21-year-old shortstop with the New York Giants. Honus recounts here the details of an "intentional" bonehead play that the fans never caught on to. Heinie Wagner had career highs of .274, 68 RBIs, and 75 runs scored for the World Champion 1912 Red Sox. His playing career ended in 1918, but he coached the Red Sox from 1921 until 1930, when he became manager for a year. (George Brace Photo Collection)

The next day the newspapers even accused him of pulling a bone. As a matter of fact, his smart thinking prevented a double play. Wagner was called out for being hit by a batted ball, of course. But that had prevented a double play, and the batter was credited with a hit. Under the rules, you know, if a base runner is hit by a batted ball he is out, and the batter gets a hit.

Nobody ever stopped to think that Heinie Wagner had figured out that situation in a flash and had solved it. Instead, they called him a bone.

HE HAD IT ALL DOPED OUT

Fred Merkle will go through life being called a bonehead simply because of his failure to touch second in that famous game with the Cubs. In 1913, in the last game of the world's series, he was again called a bone for attempting a play that was really a clever piece of thinking that didn't go through. He was merely the victim of hard luck. Fred Merkle is one of the smartest men playing baseball.

In that particular game Merkle was badly crippled, but managed to go through on one good leg. Murphy was on third and Baker at the bat in the last inning.

Baker hit a hot grounder to Merkle, who fielded the ball cleanly. He then made a bluff throw to stop Murphy and did so. It was his purpose then to touch Baker as he passed, and finally make a real throw for Murphy, getting both men. It was a quickly thought out play. But it went wrong.

After bluffing Murphy back to the bag Merkle turned to touch Baker, who was coming on top of him. On account of Merkle's crippled condition, Baker dodged him and got to the bag safely. In the mix-up Murphy made a new start and got home.

Everybody called Merkle a bonehead and the newspaper writers did a lot of kidding about it. Ball players, though, appreciated that Merkle had attempted to make a wonderfully smart play—one that would have gone through nine times out of ten.

I don't want to get in any argument with my newspaper writing friends, but they do many a ball player wrong when they roast him about something they don't understand. Those boys can pull bones just the same as ball players.

I had a chance one day in Pittsburgh to see a ball game played between the scribes out at Schenley Park. The manager of one of the teams was crazy to win and was trying to be a strict general like he thought McGraw or Fred Clarke might be.

DID HE TAKE CHANCES?

His side had the bases full and this manager got so eager that he reached over to the runner on first and hissed in his ear.

"Steal second. Go on, steal it!"

"I can't," said the other newspaper player. "There is a man already on second."

"Never you mind. I am the manager. You do what I say. Go on. Steal that bag."

The runner hesitated again.

Fred Merkle is famous for his "bonehead" play on September 23, 1908, which resulted in a tie that cost the New York Giants a critical victory. The Chicago Cubs won the pennant when the game was replayed at the end of the season. The play involved Merkle's failure to touch second base, which caused a run to be cancelled and produced the tie ending. Merkle, who was only 19 years of age at the time, went on to a 16-year Major League career with a lifetime batting average of .273. (National Baseball Hall of Fame Library, Cooperstown, New York)

"Run, or I'll knock your block off and shove you off that bag."

With that this smart manager threw a handful of dirt at his runner and shoved him off the bag. He started all right.

Well, you should have heard the uproar. But when the commotion was over and the ball had been thrown wildly four or five times the three runners had scored.

Now, I ask you, would you call that a bonehead play, or would you give the manager credit for taking chances? I'll say he took 'em, all right.

I saw Bill Hinchman called a bonehead in a game at Pittsburgh one day for really carrying out his end of a smart play.

We were playing against the Phillies and Alexander was pitching. Hinchman laid on the ball for three bases and, with one out, it looked like a good chance for a score. Hinchman got the sign for the squeeze play.

To work a squeeze play properly the man on third starts for the plate with the pitcher's swing. Alexander had caught the sign, or had outguessed us, and deliberately pitched out to Killefer, the catcher.

When Killefer turned to throw, Hinchman, of course, was fifteen feet off third base. He had started home. As a result he was caught flat-footed.

"Oh, you bone!" screamed the fans.

Just then Killefer turned loose the ball and it was a wild peg far over the third baseman's head. Hinchman came on home and scored.

"Oh, that lucky break!" cried the fans.

WHAT WOULD HE DO WITH IT?

The next day the newspapers even had fun with Hinchman for pulling a bone and being lucky enough to score on it. All he had done was to go through with the squeeze just as he had started. Naturally, he was off the bag. He had to be. The fans and experts never stopped to figure it out that the squeeze play was on and that Hinchman was playing it properly, even if Alexander didn't get on to it.

Talking about real bone plays, though, I saw a base-runner on one of the National League clubs try to steal a base in the ninth inning when there were two out and the team was eight runs behind. Can you beat that one? We all asked him what he would have done with the base if he had stolen it. One run didn't amount to anything. It would take nine to win. Why put the side out? "Don't know?" he admitted, "but that base looked so big down there I just thought I'd steal it."

I saw another base-runner try to steal home when the bases were full and there were two out and there were two strikes and three balls on the batter. That I would regard as the champion bone.

There have been several instances where a runner tried to steal third base with the bases full. A fellow once did that when Arlie Latham was standing on third. He looked down and saw the other base-runner sliding into his legs.

"Hey, get t' 'ell out of here," he said, kicking at the bone-headed runner. "Where'd you come from?"

This is not exactly a bone, but it's odd: I saw Pete Browning drop to his knees in trying to dodge a wild pitch one day when his bat, coming around the wrong way, hit the ball down the left foul line for a two-base hit.

Why Baseball Has Developed in Thirty Years

• • •

Since the first chapter of baseball reminiscences began to appear I have received hundreds of letters asking whether I think the game has improved since I started in some thirty years ago. A lot of these questions, especially those from the old-timers, are asked in an argumentative way.

Certainly baseball has improved. To one who has any powers of observation at all, the development of baseball has been remarkable. Those old-timers who have failed to see improvement are either prejudiced or have not kept their eyes open.

For example, when I first broke in, the bunt, the sacrifice and the swinging bunt were looked upon as a novelty and given the razz by most of the fans and spectators.

In 1897 the catcher stood far back, allowing the ball to hit the grandstand, until there were runners on base. A foul ball was out on the first bounce then. It seems funny now when I remember how the catcher used to stand waiting for the ball to bounce.

In those days the game was much rougher. The umpires could not and did not enforce discipline as they do now. It was not uncommon then for the spectators to get out on the field and mix up in the arguments. In most of the cities there was no such thing as fairness. Ball players took every advantage they could and the worst they got the more the fans urged them on.

The gloves we wore were not much protection. I often padded mine with duck feathers. The catchers had no protection at all for their legs. In those days the basemen should have had their legs protected. Runners thought nothing of stepping on the basemen or bumping them off the base. Everything went that a fellow could get away with. Several of the first basemen had a trick of sticking pins into a runner so to make him turn the wrong way or run out of line.

DISCIPLINE IS TIGHTENED

The biggest and most important development in baseball, to my mind, was moving the grandstands back farther so that the spectators would not be right on top of the players. Then players were taught not to talk back to spectators. As things went along, the necessity of discipline became more apparent even to the players, and the umpires were given more power. They demanded and got more respect. The improvement was gradual, but certain, in every direction.

Back in 1897 there was no rule calling a foul a strike. A player could stand up and foul them off as long as he wanted to. Occasionally an umpire with unusual nerve would call a strike on a batter for delaying the game, but they would never call a third one.

McGraw was an artist at fouling balls off. So was Roy Thomas. Those fellows could foul the ball all day if they wanted to. This wore down the pitchers and got on the crowd's nerves. The games were much longer and more tiresome.

The adoption of the foul-strike rule and the shortening of the games were big steps forward. A foul tip, though, was always a strike. That gave the chance for another trick—that of the catcher's tipping the bat. Often they wore a rubber band around the palm of their hands and would snap it so as to make the umpire think the ball had tipped the bat. He would call a strike.

Now all that has been done away with. It is foolish to say that baseball has not improved. It developed right along with the development of the players' brains. As soon as they began to realize that it was a business and that they would not last long, they started to think. That thinking competition built up the game more than any other one factor.

The introduction of the bunt, the sacrifice and so on were the direct result of the old rule allowing the catcher to stand back. The old Baltimore Orioles developed those plays first. At any rate they were the first I ever saw pull them.

SOMETHING YOU DON'T SEE

They discovered that with the catcher back, a ball dropped in front of the plate would be safe because nobody could field it. When they first started doing that the result was really funny. You modern-day fans probably never saw a big catcher running fully twenty feet to the plate trying to field a bunt and the pitcher running in from the other direction.

That play naturally brought on the sacrifice hit. Then the swinging bunt.

When this idea began to take hold, the catchers saw that the only way to offset it was to come up when they saw a foxy batter coming to the plate. In turn that brought about a change in the rule where the catcher must stay up all the time. That, naturally, shortened the game. There I have given you an illustration of how the game has developed.

When the players gradually found it to their advantage to think out new offensive and defensive plays, the development of their thinking capacity made them see how foolish it was to always quarrel with umpires and spectators. They could much better spend their time in improving their game. After all, it was the baseball playing that counted.

The newspapers joined in the development by printing fairer stories of the games. Instead of being rabid fans, the reporters got to where they looked on it as a scientific contest. They told of the new plays and praised the smart work of the players. That made the players want to be smarter. The spectators, in this way, were gradually educated into appreciating the game for its science, rather than as a battle where everybody could take a hand.

In other words, baseball developed by educating itself. It developed just like young countries do—by instruction and a matching of brains.

As baseball got to be more of a serious profession to the players than a scrap, they were not so excited in their efforts. The spectators also took it more calmly and were more critical even of their own team.

MORE APPRECIATION TODAY

I can well remember the time when such a thing as a home crowd applauding a visiting player for a great play was unheard of. In some cities a man who did that would have been considered disloyal to his home town. The sportsmanship of it never occurred to anybody. They didn't want to see a good ball game. No, they wanted to see the home club win and at any cost.

The first two cities where the crowds were inclined to show fairness toward the visiting players were New York and Boston. To this day there are some cities where the crowd will not give a visiting player credit for fine work.

In New York they seem to look on a ball game just as they would an outdoor theatrical performance. They applaud everything that is good whether it be a play by the home club or the visitors. Boston is a little more reserved and dignified, but they always give the visiting player the credit that is due him.

I always liked to play before crowds in those two cities. I was always treated royally and good-naturedly. They might josh me but it was done in good humor.

Another development was in the umpires. At first they understood their business to be merely the deciding of plays. They had to show great nerve at times, especially when there was a close one at the plate against the home club. They did not have protection from the police and you couldn't blame them for looking out for themselves.

Gradually it dawned upon these umpires that they were masters of the field, and that a most important part of their duty was to have the game run off snappily and orderly. They were responsible to the public for the game being presented properly. Their duties developed into a sort of stage direction. They had to put on a ball game just like a stage director does a show. They represented the dignity of the league. They know that now.

Has it improved? Well, I should say so!

There Was Teamwork
in Those Days

• • •

Teamwork does not appear to me as good now as in the days of the old Baltimore Orioles, the Pirates of 1901-02-03, the Giants of 1905 and the Cubs. If you have followed baseball closely you probably have noticed that no real sentiment of greatness has been thrown around a club since the Frank Chance Cubs finally petered out.

That means to me that teamwork has lost prestige in the face of individual greatness of certain players. There is a mighty good reason for this.

In a previous article I showed where baseball has developed wonderfully despite what the old-timers say. In that very development, the game has grown into such a great business that a certain group of players, working as a machine, cannot stand out for a long time. The clubs are so much larger that the same men do not work together as often.

In the old days, we were sometimes lucky enough to get together ten or twelve men who made a wonderful machine and stuck together. They had their whole heart set on winning and they overcame many difficulties that do not face ball players today. In other words, the machines do not have to be as perfect and compact now.

It has been but a few years that ball clubs have had trainers, rubbers, club doctors and all that. In our days it was largely up to each player to take care of himself. We sometimes went a whole season without getting a rubdown or massage. We were allowed to eat and train as we pleased and it was up to each man to make the best of it. To beat the game was more of an individual job.

It may sound funny for me to say it, but I agree with men like Ed Barrow, John McGraw, Billy Murray, George Stallings and many others, who think that baseball has developed entirely too much of what is called gentlemanly sportsmanship. That alone has changed baseball a lot.

NO PINK TEAS THEN

In the old days, for instance, the players did not meet at the plate and shake hands and then talk about social affairs. They were up there to fight to win and all friendship ceased the minute we got on the diamond. We looked upon all members of the opposition as enemies and knew they would take advantage of us at the slightest opportunity. Any kind of a trick was considered legitimate. There was none of that pleasant visiting to and from the benches. If a player came around our bench a few years ago the best he got was a razzing.

As a matter of fact, I think the public likes that fighting spirit. That sportsmanship is all right in football and tennis, but in baseball the spectators want to see a scrap. They want to think that the two teams have it in for each other and will give no quarter.

The tendency toward sportsmanship has made players broader minded. They look upon a ball game as merely an afternoon's sport. In our days to give quarter or cede the slightest point was like giving up our life's blood. That is why the teams have lost their compactness.

I know it is high-minded and generous for players to be considerate of each other but, to save my life, I can't look on it as old-fashioned, scrapping baseball. We used to fight right on through with crippled legs, spike wounds and everything rather than get out of the game. Nowadays ball players are protected and cared for as if they were hothouse plants.

I've seen ball players take desperate chances in my day that would not be dreamed of now. Take Frank Bowerman, the old Giant catcher, for instance. He was a ball player who could take more physical punishment than any man I ever saw. Spike cuts and bumps on the head rolled off him like water off a duck's back.

One day at the old Exposition Park in Pittsburgh when the Pirates and Giants were fighting for the championship back in 1905 and 1906, a foul fly was hit near the Pittsburgh bench. Bowerman, who was catching, ran right into the Pirate bench and hit a 4-by-4 upright that held up one end of the roof of the bench. He came with such force that he broke up this big piece of timber and bounced back four feet. But he caught that foul ball. What's more, he never let on that the bump had even hurt him.

BOWERMAN BUTTS A BARREL

During another game in that same park the crowd had overflowed and was lined up around the plate and down the foul lines. Someone had brought out a barrel for a woman spectator to sit on. She was sitting there enjoying the game when another foul fly was hit. Bowerman started for it and ran slap into the barrel, knocking it over and upsetting the woman. Evidently he had not seen her at all. He was so sore at missing the foul that he kicked the big barrel about ten feet.

"Hey, Frank," Matty, who was pitching, yelled to him, "keep your head up."

He couldn't make Bowerman understand, so Matty left the box, walked through the crowd, straightened up the barrel and lifted the woman on it. Then the game went on.

Bowerman never thought of getting hurt. Bouncing a ball off him was like hitting an iron safe. He would start for a bunt the instant he saw the batter make a move as if to dump the ball. Sometimes the ball would hit him on the leg or on the bare hands and often he would run right into the bat. Even that did not faze him. His sole idea was to get the jump on the bunted ball. Often he would make plays that otherwise would have given the pitcher and the third baseman trouble.

Bowerman would also take dangerous chances in touching base runners coming into the plate. He would slide into them head-first whether they were coming in spikes first or not. I have had several hard collisions with him. But I never saw him badly hurt. At any rate he would never let on.

Frank used to run over the bats, into the dugouts, into the stands or anywhere to get a foul ball. I often have wondered why he never got killed. But he is just as healthy and strong as ever. Bowerman runs a big dairy farm up in Michigan today. They say he is almost white-haired, but is just as hard and rough physically as ever.

YOUNGSTERS NURSED MORE NOW

Another thing that has tended to weaken the several teams as machines is the fact that it is much easier for youngsters to break in now. In the early days we did not carry so many men and each member of the team fought to hold his job against all comers. A youngster had to be a bearcat to displace some veteran then. They didn't keep him around and gradually try him out either. If he had something he had to show it right then. A player would be signed tonight and the crowd would expect him to be in the game tomorrow. If he didn't make good, he was on his way in a very short time.

But baseball machines have to be built very carefully now and they have to be kept up to a certain standard. A youngster is kept for a year or more for development. As one player weakens and drops out another is ready to put in his place. It is like keeping up a big corporation. More attention is paid to organization than merely to holding together a small gang of fighting ball players.

I don't want to be a gloomy prophet, but I don't expect to ever see any more unique teams like the old Orioles, the Pirates, the Giants or the Cubs.

The game has been considerably weakened by the pitchers being barred from certain deliveries, such as the spitball, the shine ball, the emery ball and so on.

This naturally helps the batters. It is easier to be a great hitter nowadays. You can see that by looking at the official records. Where we used to have six or seven men hitting over .300, we now have fifty or sixty.

The Shortstop's Job
and How to Fill It

• • •

Several college coaches have been complimentary enough to request that I devote an article to my ideas on how to make plays at shortstop. Before doing so though, I want to give the college boys another block of the examination questions that I gave at Carnegie Tech.

These questions are not to be answered directly. You will do better by discussing them. The answers may vary according to the situation. By keeping them in mind and studying them, I think the college teams now in formation will derive some benefit.

Defense Against Stealing Bases

1. Is the defense for stealing stronger now than in former years? Why?
2. Do you have a catcher or other infielder giving signal to the pitcher when the runner is taking too much of a lead?
3. Does your catcher signal for a waste ball when the runner has big lead in order to throw the runner out?
4. When a runner on second indicates that he will try to steal, or actually does start, does your shortstop inform the third baseman?
5. What percentage of men do you estimate are successful in stealing?
6. Which man is in the best position to receive the throw from the catcher, second baseman or shortstop?
7. In what do you most expect a man to steal?
8. What defense do you use when you expect a steal of home?

Rather than answer those questions directly I would have the college players discuss them and arrive at their own conclusions. It will be of much more benefit than the mere reading of questions and answers. Fellows forget things that do not require any thought on their own. When I studied arithmetic I remember I never could get the idea down right when the answer was given with the problem.

LEARN WHERE BATTERS HIT

Now, the most important principle I learned when I first came in from the outfield and started playing shortstop was where to place myself for certain batters. It doesn't take long to learn in what direction a certain batter usually hits. The hard job is to remember each one of the batters. A shortstop must also remember in what direction a batter hits certain pitches. Most of them will hit a curve outside to one field and a fast one to another.

This makes it all important that the shortstop know exactly what the pitcher is going to do each time. He can do this by keeping his mind on the game and his eye glued on the catcher's signals.

Now, for example, if a right-handed batter, who usually hits to left field, is up and the pitcher gives him a ball inside the plate—close to him—then I, as shortstop, would set my body so as to leap to my right, toward third base. By being in position to make a quick start the shortstop gains a full step on the ball. He makes hard chances look easy. In other words, he has outfigured the ball. An infielder should never let the ball play him.

This getting yourself placed makes a mighty big difference. If the batter should hit a ground ball, for instance, it will be right at the shortstop nine times out of ten. If he should stand flatfooted and not know in which direction he intended to start, the shortstop would be out of luck. His start must be with the crack of the bat. Otherwise he is not a big league shortstop.

Now, if the pitcher throws the ball outside of the plate—away from the right-handed batter—the shortstop must be ready to jump to his left with the crack of the bat. Nine times out of ten the batter will hit that ball toward right field. If he hits a grounder the chances are it will go between shortstop and second base or directly over the bag. If it goes further than that the second baseman can get it. But remember, the second baseman is also playing the game. He has set himself to get far around toward first base.

By anticipating a ground hit like that, the shortstop often gets credit for marvelous stops of balls hit directly over second. As a matter of fact they are not hard. The shortstop, having anticipated the play, is over there with a leap or two. He has made the hard chance easy.

LAJOIE WAS THERE FIRST

I suppose you who are old fans remember how easy all chances use to look to Napoleon Lajoie. Often he made stops that did not get applause because they looked so easy. Other players who had to race for the ball would be applauded for making phenomenal stops. That was because Lajoie figured out where the ball would probably go and always was right on top of it.

These simple directions, naturally, are simply reversed for a left-handed hitter. In either case, however, the shortstop must always be in position to go in for a slow hit ball. In other words he mustn't start too quick. Otherwise the batter might cross him. Study how to time your movements and never be so over-anxious as to let everybody on the field know what you intend to do.

Some batters are liable to hit any kind of pitched balls in any direction. Those are very difficult to play but, luckily for the infielders, there are very few of them. Still, if everything could be figured out exactly there wouldn't be any thrills in baseball. Surprise and unexpected things make the game what it is.

The shortstop in fielding a ball to his extreme right must be sure to put himself in position to throw to first base as the ball hits his hands. As his back is turned to the bag when he swings to make the play he must have a good line in his mind on where the bag is. You see, he must throw with the same motion that he fields the ball and he hasn't time to take aim. If he does the batter will beat the ball.

A fine piece of fielding was done by Frank Frisch in the last world's series, but the spectators, missing the real point of greatness, applauded his catch rather than his throw.

FRISCH'S RAPID FIRE SHIFT

With a man on third a Texas leaguer was hit back of second. It looked impossible, but Frisch started for it. On the last of two jumps he saw he would get the ball and he knew that he would have to make a throw to the plate. He suddenly shifted and jumped to the other side of the ball, so that when he caught it he could peg to the plate without turning again or looking. Can you imagine a man thinking that fast in a situation like that?

But Frisch made the catch and also nailed the runner who tried to score on the play. It was a great catch but a greater throw.

Now on a slow hit ball the shortstop must learn how to throw accurately while still on the run. It takes long practice to get that. Handling balls of this kind makes it necessary for him also to learn to field a ball with one hand and throw with the same motion. He must learn to throw from any position and get the ball away quickly. If he has to straighten up to throw a runner out at first he will never make a big league shortstop.

This thing of infielders stumbling into the ball and having a lot of luck is mostly bunk. Usually they have figured it that way. There is some luck, of course, but it usually breaks about even.

Taking throws from the catcher or other players, for that matter, is an entirely different subject. The shortstop also has to learn that part of his job and learn it well. I will have to go into that more fully in another article.

The main idea is always to give the runner half of the bag to touch. You can determine which to give him the moment the ball starts. Be careful not to hog the whole bag. It is not so much that you want to be fair as that you don't want to get your leg cut off. In this day and time a runner knows his rights and won't hesitate to take all that is coming to him.

Some More Tips
on Defense

• • •

My posing as a baseball school-master is sure to give some of the old-timers a laugh, but as long as I've started, I've got to go through with it. Maybe, at that, I'll help some young player to get started right.

Before winding up my views on how to play shortstop, I want to present one more block of questions for discussion among the amateurs.

GENERAL INFIELD DEFENSE

1. With a man on first and third, double steal being attempted, do you have the catcher pegging straight through?
2. Do you have the second base-man or shortstop covering second on sacrifice bunts with a runner on first?
3. With runner on second and sacrifice bunt used do you have your first baseman com-ing in, pitcher fielding all to his right and third baseman playing the bag?
4. Would you have the pitcher pitch a good strike when expecting a sacrifice bunt?
5. Do you find the hit-and-run played more on the first pitched ball than any other? Why?

Those should not be so hard to answer. I will not give my answers, because I think they will be more valuable as remind-ers to keep the college player thinking.

In my last article I promised that I would go on with my dis-cussion of how the position of shortstop should be played. I had got to the part concerning taking throws and touching the runner.

As I intimated, don't attempt to be smart and block base runners off the bag. If you do you won't play shortstop long. Give them half the bag in a sense of fairness as well as a sense of safety.

Knows the Route

A shortstop knows where the ball will be thrown the moment it starts. So, using that as a guide, he can determine which side of the bag to give the runner. That makes it easy to touch him, because he will surely slide for the open side. If you attempt to block him he is liable to get away with a hook slide.

If a shortstop fails to touch the runner as he comes in, he should never go after him again unless he over-slides. You've always got a chance of the umpire failing to see that you missed him, but if you try to touch him a second time it is a cinch that the umpire will call him safe. It is important that a young shortstop learn to touch the runner with the same motion that he catches the ball. The touch must be made quick and snappy.

The double play is the most important play in baseball. Short-stops and second basemen who are weak at this never last in the big league.

In making a double play when taking the throw at second base, the shortstop should always step into the diamond as he makes his throw to first. This gives him a free hand and prevents being run into by the runner. If the play is close and the runner deliberately tries to block a shortstop, the latter always has his right arm free for a throw if he steps in instead of standing still.

Now, if the ball is hit to the shortstop and he has to start the double play, his most important move is the way he throws the ball to the second baseman. It isn't enough to toss it so he can catch it. The expert shortstop tosses the ball so that the second baseman can make a free throw to first. The best way to do this is to toss the ball underhanded, chest high and directly over the bag, not where you see the baseman standing. If the shortstop tosses the ball low or too far over, the second baseman loses time in stooping and coming up to make the throw.

In taking a throw from the catcher on the double steal, it depends entirely on the start and speed of the runner on third base whether he starts for home or whether he holds his base. The shortstop must figure this out in a fraction of a second and determine whether he should stay on the bag and take the throw or whether he should run in and take it. If he goes in he is after the man on third and must forget the other.

BUSIEST BIRD DOG OF ALL

A shortstop must learn to hold base runners close to the bags by letting them know that he is watching them. By doing this carefully he can keep them back on every pitch.

It should be the duty of the shortstop to take all possible throws at third base from the outfield. This enables the third baseman to do the backing-up along with the pitcher.

The shortstop really has more duties than any man on the infield. He was originally called shortstop because he was supposed to be a help to the outfield as well as the infield. In other words, he is a short fielder. In some cities they still call him that.

The expert shortstop goes out and relays throws from the outfield. This is one of the most important duties, especially if he has a good arm. If he hasn't a good arm he has no business in the big league.

Dave Bancroft, who manages the Braves this season, is as good a man as I ever saw in cutting off throws from the outfield. He won a game in the world's series two years ago that way. There was a man on first and one on third when a single was hit to the outfield. The throw started for third base, supposedly, with no chance of getting the runner. Instead, it went to Bancroft, who had placed himself for it. He let the first runner go on to third, but turned and whipped the ball to second, getting the batter who had tried to stretch the hit. That wasn't new at all—it is often done—but it illustrates what I mean about playing the position.

If a shortstop keeps his head on his job and watches the base runners closely, he will soon learn to judge their speed and how they slide. By watching their mannerisms he can also get a pretty good line on when they intend to steal.

Batter Has Eyes, Too

A shortstop, especially in the big leagues, must watch himself all the time so as not to tip the batter off when he intends to cover the second baseman. Remember, the batter is just as smart and is also watching him. Once he discovers that the shortstop intends to cover the bag, he is likely to give the hit-and-run sign and hit the ball right through that position. That always makes an infield look foolish. A shortstop should always hold his position to see if the batter is going to hit on that particular pitch—then jump with the swing of his bat. If he doesn't swing, jump toward second.

A shortstop should never think about making errors. He should go after everything possible. Often you will knock down hits that look impossible to stop. Errors are part of the game, so do not be afraid of making them.

These views on the position of shortstop also apply to the second baseman in a general way. The main difference is that the second baseman does not have to have as long a throwing arm.

One piece of advice that I would like to give to college players and other amateurs is to forget that idea that there are such things as natural born ball players. There are no such things, no more than there are natural born steel magnates and bank presidents. You've got to learn your job by hard work, steady thinking and constant practice.

It has been said of me that I was a natural born ball player, but the fellows who made that crack probably never knew how hard I worked and how I studied to keep track of my opponents. Honestly, I have worked one solid hour at a time in the morning trying to overcome a fault I had in touching runners or in handling slow-hit balls. If you are going to be a ball player, be a good one, whether you intend doing it for a living or not.

Doping Out the Bad Balls

• • •

I reckon I set myself up to be shot at when I started this telling of my baseball days. So I guess I've got to take my medicine. You know how it is.

So many odd questions have been popped at me through the mails that they've got me winging. An old friend of mine out here in Carnegie, I guess, called the turn.

"Honus," he said, "you want to remember that when you took up that writin' business they had two strikes on you before you started."

On top of the pile, as I write, is one from a Mr. Hawley in Portland, Oregon, who asks: "How was it you struck at so many bad balls in your time and still managed to hit them? You tell young players to pick out good ones."

Mr. Hawley has got me right, at that. I reckon I did hit at more bad balls than any man in the business. I had my own system about that—one that I would not advise others to follow.

Whenever a pitcher made me look foolish on a pitch, whether it was high, low, outside or inside, I figured it out that he would be sure to give me another just like it. If I made a sucker out of a batter on a certain ball, I certainly would hand him another. So that's the way I figured they would do.

And sure enough I would call the turn nine times out of ten. Having set myself for a ball high over my head, for example, I would naturally be ready if the pitcher tried to repeat. Being set for a certain ball, I could sock it. If he shifted I would wait. I knew he would try to make me look foolish again, sooner or later.

It would be just the same as if I was looking for one over the middle. As long as a batter is looking for a certain kind of ball and gets it, he can plaster it whether it is high, low inside or outside. That, I hope, explains why I had the reputation of going after all kinds of wild pitches.

The next writer, a Mr. Ironton of New Orleans, wants to know what I considered my greatest batting accomplishment, the one that gave me the most satisfaction.

THE FAN CHIRPED, THEN . . .

My greatest accomplishment, I believe, was in the game between Louisville and Pittsburgh when I got two home runs and two singles, just when the fans were giving me the razz and begging Pittsburgh to take me back home.

The one that gave me the greatest satisfaction, though, was in the deciding game of the world's series between the Detroit Tigers and the Pirates. This game was played at Detroit in 1909.

In the sixth inning we got two men on base and I was next up. The Detroit fans and players had been giving me a terrible razz. It seems that they had never seen me play out there and, I reckon, were sort of disappointed. You know how it is—it's mighty tough on a ball player who has hit so well that fans expect him to plaster one every time he comes to bat. It's harder on him than on a player who hasn't been boosted so much in the newspapers.

Well, I came up and on the second ball pitched got it squarely on the nose and slammed it to the fence for three bases, scoring the runners. I am sure that wallop gave me a better feel than any one I ever hit.

I remember one fellow in particular who sat just back of the Detroit bench.

"It's all right," he yelled to the pitcher, "that Dutchman has got a yellow streak. Let's go!"

Just then I smacked the old onion. Only a ball player can exactly understand how I felt.

As a matter of fact we didn't need the runs, but it was those that gave us a start. The final score of the game was Pittsburgh 8, Detroit 0.

So many of the fans who have been good enough to read what I have written have asked odd questions about queer pitching and oddly pitched games that I will answer them all in one lump. I reckon that will be about the best way.

The most peculiar and surprising pitching that I ever saw in a ball game was done by Christy Mathewson in a game at the old Exposition Park in Pittsburgh, when the Giants and Pirates were fighting it out for the pennant. Matty was at his best then.

A GAME WITHOUT ONE CURVE

In the very first inning he started whipping fast balls at our batters and not one of us could touch him. Not once did he give me a curve or a slow ball, or even his fadeaway. Every time I came up it was a fast—and gee, it had smoke!—zip! zip! zip!—just like that.

"What's he using?" I asked Claude Ritchey when I came back to the bench.

"All he's pitched to me is a fast ball every time," said Claude.

"That's all I've seen, too," Fred Clarke agreed.

As the game went along we talked and talked, trying to get a line on what the big fellow had.

After we were shut out and went to the clubhouse we checked with every batter. Not one of them had seen anything but a fast ball. In other words, Mathewson had pitched an entire nine innings without offering anything like a curve. He had got away with his fast one to start on and kept right at it.

I think that is the only ball game ever pitched in which the pitcher did not use a curve or a slow ball at any time in the game.

Matty, you know, often changed his system. If he started in making some batter bite at his big loop curve he would keep right on tossing it until somebody got hold of it. Anything that was going good was good enough for Matty. He never experimented unless in a hole. But let me tell you something! When that old boy got in a hole he sure could bear down on the old apple, as ball players have a way of saying. They never made any better pitchers than Mathewson.

The hardest luck game I ever saw was pitched by McIntyre one day when we were playing the Dodgers at Brooklyn.

FIVE HIT IN ELEVENTH

For nine innings he didn't allow anything that looked like a hit, but unfortunately the Brooklyn club could not make a run and the game

From 1897 to 1915, Fred Clarke was Honus Wagner's manager and team-mate, both in Louisville and Pittsburgh. With 2,672 career hits and 1,602 managerial wins, Fred Clarke excelled both as a player and manager. He batted above .300 in eleven seasons and retired with a lifetime batting average of .312. A full-time player-manager in sixteen of his nineteen seasons as manager, Clarke led his clubs to fourteen first-place division finishes. He also led the Pirates to the first modern World Series in 1903. Clarke was inducted into the Hall of Fame in 1945. (National Baseball Hall of Fame Library, Cooperstown, New York)

went into extra innings with the score 0–0. McIntyre kept right on polishing us off in the tenth. At the end of that inning everybody was talking about McIntyre having pitched a no-hit, ten-inning game, which we thought would sure be a record.

We managed to get our first hit in the eleventh and we finally beat him, 1–0, in the thirteenth inning.

When a pitcher can pitch a ten-inning, no-hit game and then get beat, I consider that the champion hard luck of the world.

I believe Leon Ames once pitched a nine-inning no-hitter at the Polo Grounds and got beat. George Wiltse later pitched a ten-inning no-hitter.

Old Iberg [*sic*],* to my way of thinking, had the oddest delivery of any pitcher in the world. He often pitched slow balls and curves fifteen feet high between the pitcher's box and the plate, dropping them right over the pan. How he did that I was never able to figure.

Jim Vaughan had no preliminary action at all in the box. He took no wind up at all—simply stood straight up and snapped the ball at the batter as if he was handing him something.

Kantalehner always dropped his arm low behind him and looked exactly as if he were lifting a ton of lead before each delivery. I used to grunt with him. I'd feel like I was getting tired myself. Old Kanty's delivery was about as odd as any of them.

Al Demaree delivered a ball to the batter exactly as if he was putting the shot. It was mighty hard to figure what he was doing.

Carl Mays, I think, has the oddest underhand delivery of them all. Often his arm is so low that his knuckles graze the ground.

• • •

*Herman Edward "Ham" Iburg (1877–1945); Played one season in the major leagues (1902) for the Philadelphia Phillies.

Picking the Greatest
Players of All Time

• • •

In my next chapter I intend to present what I think should be the grand all-American team of all times. As a preliminary, though, I want to lay before you a list of great baseball men, including managers, so that you will have something to go on in case you do not agree with me.

This thing of picking out the very best players you have seen in thirty years is no easy job. I hope you will believe me when I tell you that I have spent one solid week selecting the different players, and then going over them again to see if I made mistakes in judgment. Often I have made changes. Little things crop up like a man's natural aggressiveness, for instance, or his great ability in a pinch. These things all have to be considered. I have given up the idea of going by the records and I think any veteran baseball man would agree with me. Some of our most valuable players in winning ball

games and pennants have never had outstanding records.

To begin with, I laid out the following managers as having some claim for the job: John J. McGraw, Fred C. Clarke, Connie Mack, Frank Chance, Pat Moran, Bill Carrigan, Wilbert Robinson, George Stallings and Frank Selee.

Now, every man in that lot has some special claim to greatness. Most of them never got what was coming to them. Take Frank Selee, for instance. Very few people know that when he was breaking down through illness, he went from Boston to Chicago and started building. He laid the foundation on which Frank Chance later completed the job. Poor Frank died from his long illness and very few of the modern day fans remember him. I might say, though, that I will not make Selee my all-American manager. He was great but others are greater.

To show you that I have gone into the matter thoroughly—I think a baseball man would be a busher not to try and do the job honestly—I have divided those managers into two classes.

FOUR OF FIGHTING TYPE

McGraw, Chance, Clarke and Stallings used pretty nearly the same system. They were, and are, of the fighting type—extremely aggressive. They were great students of the game and of human nature. They always made a point of studying the weakness of every player in the league, including their own players. If it was a weakness of character or a weakness at the bat, they made no difference. They felt it their job to prey on that weakness.

These men all were builders. They worked hard with the team at hand, but in every move they were figuring on the future. In other words they built their teams two years ahead.

None of these men was ever gentle or fatherly in handling men. They were leaders who took part in the fight and made every man stand on his own. They had no patience with ball players who were not ready to start a scrap or make noise. I remember one time McGraw telling me that he had just got a tough break of luck.

"I've got four Irish ball players," he said, "who can hit and field, but not one of them ever makes a crack in the outfield that you can hear to the bench. Can you imagine Irishmen being that quiet?"

Both Stallings and Frank Chance were so aggressive that, in case an argument on the bench or in the clubhouse went too far, they were ready to settle it with their good right arms and clenched fists. Clarke also would go to the mat with anybody who felt like disputing his authority.

The players always admired these men because they knew that the manager not only knew what he was talking about, but could do the job himself if necessary. It means a lot to a ball player to know that the manager can do whatever he tells you to do. It's just the same as the army officer who wouldn't ask a private to do anything that he couldn't do, and wasn't willing to do himself, if necessary.

KIND A FELLOW SLAVES FOR

Now, Wilbert Robinson, Connie Mack and Frank Selee used another system, all about the same. They are of the gentle lovable type of men for whom men will work their heads off just because they like them—would not want to offend or disappoint them.

Those men were particularly good in handling timid young players, or the freaks who could not get along elsewhere. They made a point of finding what troubled a young fellow and nursing him along by gentleness and encouragement. Wilbert Robinson saved no less than four good players to the game by being patient and forbearing them, and there is no telling how many Connie Mack made valuable to the league.

Some players are really temperamental and get upset when ridden too hard. They are artists at heart and get discouraged when things don't break right. Robbie used to get two or three fellows like that together and take them off on a fishing or hunting trip, making them feel that they were members of the family. The boys loved Robbie so that they would do anything in the world to please him. Besides that, he always gave them some good laughs.

Frank Selee was that way and so is Connie Mack. Except when the game gets close you'd think Connie Mack a Sunday-school teacher on the bench. He is always kind and gentle and rarely ever criticizes a player harshly in front of the others. He prefers to take the boy up to his room for a nice long talk. Connie Mack was one of the few managers who could keep Rube Waddell for any length of time. At that, Waddell had Connie picking at the coverlets at times.

Pat Moran uses a system which is a combination of both those that I have mentioned. He wants fighting players and will hop on them if necessary, but at the same time he will be kind and gentle, always encouraging. Moran has the knack of knowing a good ball player when he sees him in the rough. He will worry along with him until he gets results.

HERE'S A BATCH TO PICK FROM

Bill Carrigan, of the Red Sox, was also a sort of combination of both. He was a fighter and also a diplomat. The players were very fond of Bill, but there was no time when anybody had any doubts as to who was boss of the club.

Now, in selecting pitchers, just look what I must consider:

Walter Johnson, Christy Mathewson, Grover Alexander, Cy Young, Rube Waddell, Bill Donovan, Sam Leever, Jack Chesbro, Vic Willis, Ed Walsh, Babe Adams, Miner Brown, George Mullen, Carl Mays, Amos Rusle, Wilbur Cooper, Rod Faber, Joe McGinnity and a lot of others.

Just lay all those names out and then start to sift out their strength and weakness. It's a man job, I'm telling you.

Then look at catchers:

Roger Bresnahan, Johnny Kling, Lou Criger, Buck Ewing, Jack O'Connor, George Gibson, Chief Meyers, Red Dooin, Ivy Wingo, Chief Zimmer, Jimmy Archer, Pat Moran, Walter Smith.

I'm not trying to make you think I am working so hard, but just thought you might be interested; maybe you might start picking a team yourself—and beat me, at that.

In the infield I must consider Eddie Collins, Johnny Evers, Jimmy Collins, Hughey Jennings, John McGraw, Claude Ritchey, Art Fletcher, Bobby Wallace, Tommy Leach, Herman Long, Fred Tenney, Rabbit Maranville, Frank Chance, Joe Tinker, Rogers Hornsby, Jake Daubert, Harry Steinfeldt, Frank Frisch and many others.

There isn't a bad one in the lot, is there? How would any manager in the big league today like to buy any one of those boys for $50,000.

In the outfield, my list includes Willie Keeler, Tris Speaker, Ty Cobb, Max Carey, Joe Kelley, Bill Lange, Clarence Beaumont, Frank Schulte, Hugh Duffy, Eddie Roushe, Mike Donlin, Bucky Freeman— well, that will give you an idea.

I may have left a few great ones out here, but they will appear in the teams that I pick. I know I am going to catch the devil in criticism, but I'm all set.

My Grand All-American Team

• • •

This is my selection of a grand all-American team* to represent the best there has been in baseball for the past thirty years:

Manager—John J. McGraw of New York

Captain—Fred C. Clarke of Pittsburgh

First Base—George Sisler of St. Louis Browns

Second Base—Napoleon Lajoie of Philadelphia and Cleveland

Shortstop—Bobby Wallace of the old St. Louis Browns

Third Base—Jimmy Collins of Boston

Extra Infielder—Eddie Collins of Philadelphia and Chicago

Center Field—Tris Speaker of Cleveland

Left Field—Fred Clarke of Pittsburgh

Right Field—Ty Cobb of Detroit

Extra Outfielder—Babe Ruth of New York

Catchers—Johnny Kling of the Cubs, Roger Bresnahan of the Giants, Ray Schalk of the White Sox

Pitchers—Walter Johnson of Washington, Christy Mathewson of the Giants, Grover Cleveland Alexander of the Cubs, Cy Young and Rube Waddell

Pinch-Hitters—Sammy Strang and Ham Hyatt

That team, I realize, does not agree with any of those I have seen published, as the choice of such men as John McGraw, Connie Mack and Babe Ruth. Neither does it agree with the team given in the guidebook. The lat-

• • •

*Eighteen of the twenty-one players Wagner selected in 1924 for his All-American team were subsequently elected to the Baseball Hall of Fame— not formed until 12 years later in 1936. This is certainly a strong statement on Wagner's ability in judging baseball talent.

ter, of course, is made in exact accordance with records, the human element not being taken into account.

All of these baseball men and the guidebook have been good enough to place me at shortstop, a fact that is my greatest pride in life. It is not for me to pass judgment on myself, naturally. I am limiting myself to a study of the players I have observed in action.

THEY'RE HONUS'S OWN BETS

To be prepared for a lot of argument that is sure to come, I will explain in detail why I have made these selections. I have looked over the selections of others, but in no way have I allowed them to influence me in making my own. Whether you agree with me or not, these are my selections, and like the fellow who went home to his wife with a poor alibi, I'm going to stick to them.

I have selected McGraw as manager because of his great record, and also because of his knowledge of every angle of the game, as a player as well as a manager. He knows his business. McGraw also knows how to handle men. He is a great executive as well as a field manager. At no time in his life did McGraw ever allow club owners to influence him in the signing or purchase of players. His strong will power made that possible.

With the team I have selected, however, very little managing would be necessary. All my manager would have to do would be to make out a schedule and then come around on payday. Incidentally, it would be interesting to speculate on just how much a manager would pay each of these men according to present day rates of salary. Who would get the most money?

Already I have a feeling that some of the critics will say that I have selected too many left-handed hitters. They may have an idea that this team would be weak on left-handed pitching. But I have taken that into consideration. Every man I have selected can hit left-handers as well as right-handers. I have purposely left out those left-handed hitters who have to be taken out against southpaws in a pinch. I never thought much of a ball player as a star hitter who was weak against left- or right-handed pitching. A good hitter can hit any kind. Fred Clarke, for example, was the best left-handed hitter against left-handed pitching that I ever saw.

Cy Young was perhaps the most consistent and durable pitcher in the history of the game. He won 511 games—almost 100 more than any other pitcher in history. He won 30 games in a season five times and topped 20 wins an astounding fifteen times. He pitched the first perfect game in American League history in 1904, against Connie Mack's Philadelphia Athletics. He was inducted into the Hall of Fame in 1937. After Young's death in 1955, Baseball Commissioner Ford Frick introduced the Cy Young Award for the best pitcher in baseball, voted on by the Baseball Writers Association. (George Brace Photo Collection)

Between 1896 and 1908, Sammy Strang played 10 seasons with seven different teams. In 1905 he led the National League with eight pinch hits, and baseball legend has it that his penchant for "coming through in the pinch" gave rise to the term "pinch hitter." (George Brace Photo Collection)

How the Choice Is Based

I have taken several qualities into consideration—batting, fielding, base running and love of the game. More important, however, are brains, aggressiveness, length of service and teamwork.

Now, when you consider length of service, which is probably the most important of all, you will see that this club could be kept on the field for many years without falling apart. There would be no worry about filling up weak places every year. Every one of those players not playing now lasted fifteen years or more.

I have limited myself to five pitchers because I consider that enough. All pitchers do better with plenty of work.

My reason for selecting three catchers is that I could use Bresnahan, in a pinch, as a pitcher, an infielder or an outfielder. That is also true of McGraw. Even though McGraw is my manager he could be used in the infield as a pinch-hitter or a base-runner. He is the best I ever saw to get on base either by walking, being hit by the pitcher or hitting the ball. I am assuming, of course, that all these players would be in their prime when I started my club on the field the first season. As a matter of fact some of those had retired before the others were born. I guess old Cy Young was through when George Sisler was a baby. It's sort of funny, at that, to think of old Jimmy Collins and Babe Ruth on the same team. They were putting Jimmy on the All-American teams of all time when Babe Ruth was born.

To my club I have added pinch-hitters because they are a very important part of any team nowadays. I have selected Sammy Strang and Ham Hyatt. They were the best I ever saw. Sammy made eleven pinch-hits in a row one season.

My Five Greatest Pitchers

• • •

Manager—John J. McGraw
of New York
Captain—Fred C. Clarke
of Pittsburgh
First Base—George Sisler
of St. Louis Browns
Second Base—Napoleon Lajoie
of Philadelphia and
Cleveland
Shortstop—Bobby Wallace of
the old St. Louis Browns
Third Base—Jimmy Collins
of Boston
Extra Infielder—Eddie Collins
of Philadelphia and Chicago
Left Field—Fred Clarke
of Pittsburgh
Center Field—Tris Speaker
of Cleveland
Right Field—Ty Cobb of Detroit
Extra Outfielder—Babe Ruth
of New York
Catchers—Johnny Kling of the
Cubs, Roger Bresnahan
of the Giants, Ray Schalk
of the White Sox
Pitchers—Walter Johnson
of Washington, Christy
Mathewson of the Giants,
Grover Cleveland Alexander
of the Cubs, Cy Young and
Rube Waddell
Pinch-Hitters—Sammy Strang
and Ham Hyatt

In selecting Walter Johnson, Christy Mathewson, Grover Cleveland Alexander, Cy Young and Rube Waddell as the five greatest pitchers of all time I have the following reasons:

Walter Johnson deserves extra credit for the fact that he has lasted longer than any other pitcher that I recall, excepting Cy Young. They thought Johnson's terrific speed would wear him down. But it didn't. Johnson was smart enough to see that also, and as soon as he felt the strain he shifted to other forms of pitching and saved that wonderful arm. It is still good.

Johnson had terrific speed and quick breaking curve when he broke into the league. That alone pulled him through until he began to study the art of his job. Being an intelligent fellow, Johnson soon got on to all the tricks of pitching and developed a marvelous control which enabled him to mix them up.

Johnson has the longest pitching arm in baseball. I think it is even longer than was that of Rube Waddell. He has such a tremendous reach that the batters used to say they were afraid of swinging hard for fear of hitting him on the fingers when he was turning loose his fast one. That, of course, was just baseball joshing, you know what I mean.

Johnson was always in shape and is just as crazy to win now as when he started. He knows his game thoroughly and is a good hitter and a fair fielder. Often he goes in as a pinch-hitter. Johnson is of such even disposition and so eager to give his best to the club that he is easy to handle.

Christy Mathewson, in many ways, was the smartest pitcher that ever walked on a diamond. He had a peculiar trick of being able to

Walter Johnson's sidearm fastball was in a class by itself, estimated today to have been as fast as 99 miles per hour—unheard of in his day. He fanned 3,508 batters in his 21-year career with the Washington Senators, and his 110 shutouts are more than any other pitcher. He had ten successive seasons of 20 or more victories, and his 417 career wins is second only to Cy Young on the all-time list. His ERA of 1.14 in 1913 set a record that stood for 55 years. Johnson was one of the first five players inducted into the Hall of Fame in 1936. (George Brace Photo Collection)

Christy Mathewson was the dominant pitcher of his era, winning 373 games over seventeen seasons, primarily for the New York Giants. He won at least 22 games for 12 straight years beginning in 1903 and won 30 games or more four times. Mathewson played in four World Series, winning only in 1905 when he tossed three shutouts in six days against the Athletics. He set the modern National League mark with 37 wins in 1908. In 1936, he was one of the first five players admitted to the Baseball Hall of Fame, along with Honus Wagner. (George Brace Photo Collection)

read the other fellow's mind, it seemed like. That is why he is such a great checker and bridge player. I've seen him play against eight checker players at the same time and win all the games. To do that, you know, a fellow has got to have a great memory. Do you think you could remember every move on eight different checker boards at the same time, and then call out your move on each board? I'll tell the world this Dutchman couldn't.

FIVE HITS, THEN NO MORE

Mathewson pitched baseball just like he played checkers. He knew every weakness of every batter in the league. If it was a new man he found it out in about fifteen minutes. Poor Eddie Grant used to tell about getting five hits off Matty the first time he ever faced him, and then didn't get another for the rest of the season. A lot of the boys had that experience.

Mathewson had a great fast ball with a jump on it. He had medium speed—not the tremendous smoke of Johnson and Waddell. Then he had a good slow ball, his famous fadeaway, a drop ball, ordinary curve and the spitball. I never saw him use the spitball often. But he had it when he wanted to turn it loose. That boy never overlooked anything. His greatest asset, though, was his perfect control. He delivered every pitch with exactly the same movement. To outguess him was impossible.

Mathewson always saved himself by letting his fielders do most of the work. He let them know what he would pitch and they could set themselves accordingly. He watched the bases very closely and was a wonder when it came to guessing what the other side intended to do.

Matty would go along in an easy way until his opponents got men on bases and then he would tighten up so quickly that you'd think a different pitcher had come in. He worked hard to win, whether he was pitching or not. Matty was a good fielder and a fair hitter. He was great on the coaching lines, though he never made much fuss about it. He was a big help to McGraw in coaching young pitchers, both in and out of the game.

Grover Cleveland Alexander showed me more different kinds of pitches than any man I ever faced. I used to keep a chart of the different kinds of balls the pitchers would use. Alexander led them all. He had nine different pitches.

Alexander is a big strong fellow and a willing worker. He is popular personally and as a pitcher. He has the greatest assortment of curves in the world—bar none. Alex has a fast ball, medium ball, slow ball, drop ball and a curve, all of which he can throw half side-arm or overhanded. What's more, he has a slow ball and a raise curve which he uses underhanded.

HE WATCHES EVERY BASE

Alexander has perfect control and knows how to mix them up. There is no chance to outguess him. He can make his fast ball sail, in or out to the batter. The only other pitcher I ever heard of who could sail his fast ball either way is Wilbur Cooper of the Pirates. That trick got my goat for fair the first few times I saw it.

Alex watches the bases very closely and is one of the best in calling the turn on the other side. He is a wonder at breaking up the squeeze play—so good that mighty few teams have tried it on him for the past few years. He is almost as good in breaking up the hit-and-run play. Alex is always eager to pitch just for the sport of winning. That, of course, makes him a mighty easy man for a manager to handle. He really handles himself. Alex is also easy on umpires and, as a consequence, is very popular with them. That means a lot. He never gets the worst of it.

Cy Young, my fourth right-hander, was a different type of pitcher from the others. We use to call him the curveless wonder. He had terrific speed that gave the ball a snappy jump. But his curves were little dinky affairs that didn't seem to break at all. But they broke quickly, and just enough to make the batter miss. He had a short and quick breaking drop curve that was a wonder.

Old Cy, as we called him, pitched for more than twenty years and was good all the time. He never wasted many balls, but worked the corners of the plate, making it hard on the umpire as well as the batter. Young's fastball was peculiar in that it broke in and upward as it crossed the plate.

Young was always in good shape and was allowed to use his own judgment as to how to prepare himself in the spring training period.

Grover Cleveland Alexander debuted with the Phillies in 1911, leading the league with 28 wins (a modern-day rookie record), 31 complete games, 367 innings pitched, and 7 shutouts. He dominated the National League from 1914 to 1917, leading the league in wins, with more than 30 wins three times, and winning the Triple Crown in 1915 and 1916. Alexander's 373 career wins and 90 career shutouts are both National League records. He was inducted into the Hall of Fame in 1938. (George Brace Photo Collection)

He was of powerful build and had an arm like steel. If you ever felt that arm, you wouldn't wonder why he lasted so many years as a big-league pitcher.

WADDELL USED HIS HEAD

Young never drove a batter from the plate—dusting off, ball players call it—and he seldom hit a batter. The beauty of his pitching was that the whole team could sit back and feel confident of having a well pitched game. It was just like sitting back of three aces in a poker game. No manager ever had to worry about Cy Young. He never worried umpires either.

Rube Waddell has been selected as my one left-hander because I think him the best southpaw that ever pitched a baseball. Waddell may not have known as much about his art and about things in general as the others. He did not have to. All he had to do, as we ball players have a way of saying, was to bear down on that old apple. Some writers have said that Waddell never used his head in pitching. But don't believe all of that. When Rube got in the box he knew what he was doing, make no mistake about that. Of course, it took a diplomat to handle Waddell, but it was worth it.

Waddell had terrific speed, his fast ball breaking in and upward as it crossed the plate, something like Cy Young's. He also had a good ordinary curve and a drop ball that was a beauty. He had good control for a left-hander. The beauty of having Waddell on the bench was that be wanted to pitch all the time. He was anxious to win. He never thought of himself on the field. The players could jolly him into pitching at any time or playing any other position, for that matter. He was a real good fielder and a fair hitter.

Though Waddell was hard on his manager, as a rule, he was mighty easy on umpires. He never got into trouble with them.

Rube Waddell had the largest pitching hand I ever saw. He could make his fingers meet around a baseball like you could around a pool ball. That, I think, is what gave him such terrible speed. Throwing a baseball was to him about like throwing a big marble would be to you.

Now, those are my five All-American pitchers and I don't believe you can beat them.

The Big Stars
of the Infield

• • •

HONUS'S ALL-
AMERICAN TEAM

Manager—John J. McGraw
of New York
Captain—Fred C. Clarke
of Pittsburgh
First Base—George Sisler
of St. Louis Browns
Second Base—Napoleon
Lajoie of Philadelphia and
Cleveland
Shortstop—Bobby Wallace
of the old St. Louis Browns
Third Base—Jimmy Collins
of Boston
Extra Infielder—Eddie
Collins of Philadelphia
and Chicago
Left Field—Fred Clarke
of Pittsburgh
Center Field—Tris Speaker
of Cleveland
Right Field—Ty Cobb
of Detroit
Extra Outfielder—Babe Ruth
of New York
Catchers—Johnny Kling
of the Cubs, Roger Bresna-
han of the Giants, Ray Schalk
of the White Sox
Pitchers—Walter Johnson
of Washington, Christy
Mathewson of the Giants,
Grover Cleveland Alexander
of the Cubs, Cy Young and
Rube Waddell
Pinch-Hitters—Sammy Strang
and Ham Hyatt

The main distinguishing difference between the grand all-
American infield that I have
selected and that of others is
that I have put Napoleon Lajoie
at second base instead of Eddie
Collins. Also I have put Bobby
Wallace at shortstop.

I have not done that without
good reason. I would be willing to bet on my infield just as it
stands—Sisler, Lajoie, Wallace
and Jimmy Collins, with Eddie
Collins as the extra man.

I fail to see how any baseball
man who has kept in touch with
the game could name any man
over George Sisler at first base.

Eddie Collins played
twenty-five seasons in the
major leagues, starting in
1906 with the Philadelphia
Athletics and playing for the
Chicago White Sox from
1916 to 1926. He was player-
manager of the White Sox
from August 1924 through
1926 and returned to the
Athletics from 1927 to 1930.
An excellent second base-
man, he batted over .340 for
ten seasons. Collins fin-
ished his career with 3,315
hits, 744 steals, 1,300 RBIs,
and a .333 batting average.
He won the MVP Award in
1914. Collins later coached
the Athletics and was general manager of the Boston
Red Sox from 1933 to 1947.
He was inducted into the
Baseball Hall of Fame in
1939. (George Brace Photo
Collection)

George Sisler, in many ways, is one of the most remarkable ball players that ever lived. Incidentally, he is one of the very few college boys who stepped in to take rank with the greatest the game ever produced—the Immortals, as fancy writers call them. You will notice that the college men are very, very scarce on the teams selected by various authorities on the game. I never have quite understood why a college man shouldn't be as great a ball player as the man who got his schooling on the town lot. Probably the answer is the same as that to the old gag: "Why do white sheep eat more than black sheep?" The answer being, "Because there are more of them."

Most college men are advised by their friends not to go into professional baseball. That probably explains why they are in such minority. They can do better at something else that they have been training and studying for.

Sisler is not only a great first baseman but he is just as good a pitcher. A good hitter like him cannot be wasted as a pitcher, though a pitcher is out of the batting order too much. Sisler is a wonderful natural hitter. He walked up to the plate with as much confidence the first time I ever saw him as he has done since. He can hit any kind of pitching and does it so naturally that he really makes batting look easy. His greater value is that he can hit into any field. Outfielders never know where to play for him.

Sisler is not an individual star but a great team worker. He has studied baseball from every angle and likes to play the game just for the sport of it. He is very fast on the bases and, on top of that, knows when to start. It's pretty hard for a pitcher to outguess Sisler.

But as a first baseman, Sisler is particularly good in fielding bunted balls. His great arm helps a lot. Then he is a bird on taking

George Sisler, according to Ty Cobb, was "the nearest thing to a perfect ballplayer." A college-educated engineer, Sisler was one of baseball's most intelligent and graceful players, playing for the St. Louis Browns from 1915 to 1927. He won two batting titles, batting .407 in 1920 and .420 in 1922, and also set the major league record of 257 total hits in 1920, which stood for 84 years. He hit .300 or better thirteen times and had a .340 lifetime batting average in 2,055 games. Sisler was inducted into the Hall of Fame in 1939. (George Brace Photo Collection)

Rhoderick John "Bobby" Wallace was a Major League pitcher, infielder, manager, umpire, and scout. A native of Pittsburgh, Wallace debuted in 1894 as a starting pitcher with the Cleveland Spiders and began seeing playing time in the outfield and on the mound in 1896. In 1897, Wallace became an everyday player as the Spiders' full-time third baseman, batting .335 and driving in 112 runs. He also played with both St. Louis National and American League franchises, retiring after the 1918 season with a .268 batting average, 1,059 runs, 34 home runs, 1,121 RBIs, and 201 stolen bases. Following his playing days, he also managed, coached, and umpired. He was inducted into the Baseball Hall of Fame in 1953. (George Brace Photo Collection)

low throws to first. There are many first basemen who are wonderful at getting them over their heads, but the boys who are sure shots in picking them out of the dirt are very rare.

Sisler is a real gentleman, always having consideration for his teammates as well as his opponents. That makes him easy to handle. He always keeps his head. Sisler is easy on umpires. I expect him to make a wonderful manager. He is a natural leader.

I have considered the other great ones—Jiggs Donohue, Fred Tenney, Tommy Tucker, George Kelley and all of them, but my choice must go to Sisler.

Napoleon Lajoie is my pick for second base without a moment's hesitation. I'd rather have him on my club than any man I ever saw. There was never such a hard and graceful hitter as Lajoie. What's more, there was never any better ball player. Lajoie was a man of powerful build and, though strong as an ox, he was as graceful in every move as a dancer. He swung through on a hit with as much rhythm as a professional golfer. In fielding ground balls he made them all look easy. It was the ease with which he handled his muscles that made him last so long. Very few of the critics seem to have picked out the one great point in Lajoie's hitting. He drove a ball so far, as a rule, that the outfielders played very deep for him. That made it a cinch for a runner to score from second base on a single. This is also true of Babe Ruth and I have wondered why more experts have not pointed that out as a reason for his driving in so many runs.

Lajoie had a wonderful arm and was a sure shot in relaying throws from the outfield to the plate. His quickness and grace made him a star at completing or starting double plays. Lajoie was not one of the base runners but he was a fairly good one. At any rate, he always knew what he was doing. He was steadily on the job, seldom getting injured.

AVERAGE .351 FOR 18 YEARS

Lajoie had the same hard luck as Walter Johnson in never having had a chance to play in a world's series.

Now when, in addition to these things, you recall that Lajoie had a batting average of .351 for eighteen years, you can well understand why I have picked him over all comers. I'll admit that Eddie Collins runs the big Frenchman a close second. That is why I have made Collins my utility infielder.

Bobby Wallace of the old St. Louis club is my pick for shortstop and the one thing that always has puzzled me is why Bobby never got more in the limelight. There was one of the greatest ball players in the world and the chances are that half the young fellows of today never heard of him. He was such a perfect machine. I reckon

Jimmy Collins was a highly regarded third baseman and clutch hitter, playing in Boston's National and American league teams for 12 years of his 14-year career. He batted .346 in 1897 and in 1898 led the National League in home runs with fifteen. Collins hit .300 or better five times in his Boston career and was player-manager for the first six seasons in the upstart American League Boston club. He led the Boston Americans to the World Championship in 1903. He was inducted into the Hall of Fame in 1945. (George Brace Photo Collection)

they just sort of considered Wallace as belonging at short and never thought about giving him a boost. He was so generally good as not to be noticed.

Wallace was as sure a fielder and pegger to first as ever lived. He was never regarded as a heavy hitter but he was one of the surest men in a pinch that I ever have seen. To my mind Bobby Wallace was the best shortstop we ever had on making double plays and on coming in for slow-hit grounders. He had studied every batter so that he knew where they would hit certain pitches, and he would be right on top of the ball. He was so perfect in this that a lot of folks thought him born under a lucky star. It wasn't luck at all. He had figured it out that way.

Wallace could cover as much ground, either to his right or left, as anybody—and probably more. I used to wish that I could do some of the tricks that Bobby did. He was a smart base runner and good team worker. Everybody from the manager to the bat boy liked Bobby and, consequently, he was easy to handle. Even the umpires liked him.

DREAMED OF BASEBALL

Wallace was one of those fellows who talked and thought baseball all the time. It was his fun as well as his life work. Yes, I have taken into consideration his lack of hitting, and still I select him as the grand All-American shortstop of all time.

There is not much use discussing Jimmy Collins. Every All-American team I have seen picked for the past few years had him on it. They couldn't get away from it, that's all. There has never been another Jimmy Collins. Others have come close, but he was and still is the standard. Jimmy set the model in playing third base. He invented most of the present methods of third-base play.

Jimmy was playing third when the old Orioles started the bunting plays. In a month he had solved this new style. He could beat any man in the world in starting with the bat and being on top of a bunt before it had gone thirty feet. He got to where he could scoop these bunts up with one hand and throw them to first with the same motion. On account of his deadly defense the old timers thought up the idea of bunting toward first base and drawing the first baseman off the bag.

Collins covered a lot of ground and, with his wonderful arm, could get a man from almost anywhere. As I say, he was the first player to discover the proper method of handling a bunt and every third baseman to this day copies him. Not one has ever improved on his system.

Collins was a hard hitter and a great base runner. He belongs to what I have called the aggressive type, though he attended strictly to business and laid off the umpires. Jimmy was also game. No base runner ever chased him away from the bag by coming spikes first. Yes, Jimmy Collins was the model third baseman. They are still trying to copy him, but few have succeeded.

I'll stand pat on my All-American infield.

The Catchers Who Head the List

• • •

I guess, after all, Johnny Kling of the old Cubs was the best all-around catcher I ever saw. I have put him at the top of the catching staff of my grand All-American team, and the more I think about it, the more I am convinced of being right. I have put Roger Bresnahan and Roy Schalk to work with Kling.

That, to my way of thinking, would be the best catching outfit that baseball ever has seen or, maybe, ever will see. If any baseball man doesn't agree with me I'm open to argument. I'll present mine first.

Johnny Kling was always aggressive and had the best throwing arm from any position of any catcher I ever saw. He was a wonder at finding out batters' weaknesses and was allowed to sign the pitchers as he judged best.

Kling had another faculty that I have never seen in another catcher. While warming up the pitcher before the game, he could tell which was the pitcher's best ball to pitch for that day. Did you ever know anybody else who could do that? One day a pitcher's fast ball might be best; another day it might be his curve ball or his slow ball. Kling would find out quickly and the pitcher would feature that particular ball for that day, especially in the pinches. That is one of the secrets of many a pitcher's success and also of the old Cubs' success. A batter never knew exactly how to figure the pitcher. Kling used to warm up two or three pitchers and the managers would let him make the selection for the day.

Johnny was a sure hitter and a beautiful fielder of foul flies and bunted balls. He was a wonder on tagging base runners and on backing up players at first base. Kling had a sort of knack of

It was said that Roger Bresnahan was one of baseball's most natural players and might have starred in any position. He played all nine positions
for a variety of teams during his 17-year career from 1897 to 1915. Widely
regarded as among the best catchers, Bresnahan was also an innovator,
introducing early shin-guard equipment and experimenting with a protec-
tive helmet. In 1945 Bresnahan became the first catcher to be inducted
into the Hall of Fame. (George Brace Photo Collection)

guessing on what ball a runner would attempt to steal and generally did the thinking for the pitchers.

Kling was a past master at breaking up the double steal. The fact that there was a man on third as well as first never worried him. He would whip that ball down to second just the same. Often he would freeze the man on third and then get the other runner by ten feet. That took nerve and Johnny Kling had a barrel of it. He was never excited in the least; was thinking all the time. He was a wonderful team worker and was always on the job. Yes, first prize goes to Johnny Kling.

NEVER FORGET A WEAKNESS

Roger Bresnahan runs Kling a close second. I notice that John McGraw puts Bresnahan on top because of his ability to play in any position and on account of his hitting. Bresnahan, I believe, is the only catcher who ever led on the batting list. Roger was a smart ball player, make no mistakes about that. He was particularly great on blocking runners at the home plate and was an artist on taking a throw either from the infield or the outfield.

Bresnahan was a thinking ball player. He never had to be told twice about the weakness of any batter. He had a great memory. Roger was unusually aggressive and fearless and was a good influence for young pitchers.

Roger was hard on umpires but used diplomacy at times. To this day I don't think Bresnahan believes that a called third strike on him was ever over the plate. His heart was so set on the game that he thought the umpires were giving him the worst of it—honestly thought so. He often played right on after being badly hurt. Bresnahan, incidentally, was the inventor of the present shin guards used by catchers. He used to get some bad spike wounds and thought up this idea of protecting the legs. At first he was laughed at, but you will notice that all catchers use the shin guards now.

Ray Schalk, my third catcher, is a dandy. I think him the most natural catcher of them all. He actually makes the work look easy. Schalk can catch any kind of pitching and the pitchers always want him to work with them. He has a great baseball head and knows exactly how to direct a pitcher. For a man his size Schalk has great endurance. He can catch every day during a season. Fans forget that a catcher has to make as many throws as the pitcher. That is very tiring on the arm. Still, the pitcher gets at least three days rest out of four, while the catcher sticks in there day in and day out until he gets hurt.

HE COVERS THE MOST GROUND

Schalk is good at breaking up the double-steal and squeeze play. He is always in the game and probably covers more ground during a ball game than any catcher in the business.

I have no excuse to offer for the outfield I have chosen—Cobb, Speaker, Fred Clarke and Babe Ruth—but I am down right sorry for

Ray Schalk started with the Chicago White Sox in 1912. He played with the White Sox until 1928, establishing himself defensively by leading the league's catchers in fielding percentage eight times and putouts nine times. He also became one of the finest baserunning catchers of all-time, setting a single-season stolen base record for the position in 1916 with thirty steals. Schalk played on the 1917 world champion White Sox team and was one of the honest players on the 1919 Black Sox team, hitting .304 for the series. Schalk managed the Sox in 1927 and 1928, winning 102 and losing 125 games. Schalk moved to the New York Giants in 1929, appearing in only five games before retiring. He finished his career with a .253 average, 579 runs, 11 home runs, 594 RBIs, and 177 stolen bases. He was elected to the Hall of Fame in 1955. (George Brace Photo Collection)

the number of great fellows I had to leave out. It's no easy matter for a man like me to leave off such men as Keeler, Duffy, Kelley, Beaumont and—well, a lot of them. Most of these fellows played with me at some time or other.

Ty Cobb is certainly entitled to an outfield position on account of his great hitting, base-running and general aggressiveness. In other words, Cobb comes mighty close to being the greatest ball player that ever lived. Until Babe Ruth came into the limelight, I guess Cobb was the greatest drawing card that baseball ever knew. And he never disappointed, either.

Cobb is simply a natural baseball wizard. He plays every game as if his life depended upon it. He will take any sort of a chance to win and his moves are so unexpected and daring that he keeps his opponents on the anxious seat. Many ball players have knocked Cobb for his roughness, but I never did. He took his chances and expected others to do the same. He was as game as they come.

Cobb believes in his own style of play and usually has proven that

Tris Speaker played in the American League for 22 years, beginning in 1907. His .345 lifetime batting average and defensive play made him one of Cobb's few rivals as the greatest player of the 1910s. Speaker led the league in doubles eight times and still holds the career mark with 792. His shallow play in center field enabled him to record 449 assists, placing him atop the all-time list. He was also a very successful player-manager, guiding Cleveland to a World Championship in 1920. He was inducted into the Hall of Fame in 1937. (George Brace Photo Collection)

he is right. Cobb is a dangerous man to block. He is as hard as iron and insists on getting all that is coming to him. No man was ever able to get a better lead off a base than Cobb. Once he starts he goes through. Gee, what a ball player.

Fred Clarke was not only a great fielder, but a great hitter and a natural baseball leader. He was another fearless base runner like Cobb. Men who blocked him often got hurt, but I don't think Clarke ever deliberately injured anybody. Believe me, though, he always took all that was coming to him.

A HARD LOSER BUT GAME

Clarke could hit to all fields and could hit any kind of pitching, whether it was right-handed or left-handed. He was especially good on picking out balls to hit—never went after a bad one. Clarke was a very tricky player, always taking advantage of the other fellow's weakness. He neither took nor gave quarter on the base paths. He was willing to take his chances and expected the other man to do the same.

Clarke was great on instructing pitchers. He was a hard loser and so game that he never let on when he was hurt. He played whether sick, hurt or well. He lasted for twenty years or more and seemed as good when he quit as when he started.

Tris Speaker, my third outfielder, is another of the world's great ball players. Tris in some ways is the most popular ball player in the country. Everybody likes him personally and admires his ball playing. He is a great natural hitter and probably the best ground covering outfielder that ever lived. He hits to all fields and any kind of pitching. It's almost impossible to fool Speaker on anything. He can go back farther for a fly ball than anybody and can come in as close. Speaker is always thinking baseball and keeps the other players on their toes.

No all-American team would be complete without Babe Ruth, either as a regular or extra man. His hitting alone gives him a place. And, let me tell you, Ruth is a much better fielder and a faster man on base than a lot of people think. He looks slow on account of his immense size, but that boy can get about. Babe Ruth is without doubt the longest hitter that baseball ever knew. I have seen all the long-range boys but nobody in the world could ever hit a ball like Ruth. Many pitchers are justly afraid of pitching to Ruth. They fear he may hit a ball directly back at them that would be fatal. They pass him for that reason as well as any other. If I had him in the two-three hole you can bet I'd let him walk rather than put one in the groove.

That completes my team. I'd like to see some outfit beat it.

The Best Team
I Ever Saw

• • •

One of the odd things in what you might call the literature of baseball is that the Pittsburgh club of 1901–02–03 is seldom mentioned by writers in discussing the great ball teams of past years.

I have been asked for my opinion on the subject and I come right out in the open in saying the Pirates, who won the pennants in those years, were about the best ball club I have ever seen, before or after.

I know that the Orioles were great, that the Cubs, the Athletics and the Giants were also great. I'm taking nothing away from them, but I do think the writing fellows—and that goes for the famous baseball men, too—have overlooked the one best bet.

That team was not only good enough to win three pennants, but it did it after a big slice of the stars had been taken away by the American League, just then getting its start. The Pirates of 1901 were made up of a lot of young fellows who played for the team as a whole and never thought of their personal records. It's the only ball club I ever have seen where every man could be depended upon to do his part when called on. Nobody on the club ever thought: "Now, if we only had somebody in that fellow's place." No, they thought every man on the club the right man for his job. That means a lot.

On that team it was a case of follow the leader. Fred Clarke was the leader, was playing such a whirlwind game then that he seemed to carry all the players along in the same style.

Why, on that 1901 club we lost enough good players to make up a pretty fair club in any league. Still we had the spirit and went right on winning just the same. Just by accident I have the box score of the game which decided the pennant. You might be interested in looking at it.

Here it is:

Historic Box Score from 1901

Pittsburgh	AB	R	H	PO	A	E
Davis, rf	3	0	1	3	1	0
Clarke, lf	3	1	0	2	0	0
Beaumont, cf	4	1	1	3	0	0
Wagner, ss	4	2	2	1	2	1
Bransfield, 1b	4	0	2	9	1	0
Ritchey, 2b	4	0	2	4	3	0
Leach, 3b	1	0	0	0	1	0
Burke, 3b	2	0	1	4	2	2
Kimmer, c	3	1	1	1	3	1
Phillippi, p	3	0	0	0	2	0
Totals	31	5	10	27	15	4

Brooklyn	AB	R	H	PO	A	E
Kesler, rf	5	1	0	1	0	0
Sheckard, lf	5	0	1	0	0	0
Doland, cf	4	0	2	2	0	1
Kelley, 1b	4	1	1	10	1	0
Daly, 2b	4	0	1	2	3	0
Dahlen, ss	4	1	2	5	6	1
Irwin, 3b	3	0	0	4	3	0
Farrell c	4	0	1	3	2	0
Kitson, p	4	1	2	0	1	0
Totals	37	4	10	24	16	2

Score by Innings

	1	2	3	4	5	6	7	8	9	
Pittsburgh	0	1	1	0	0	0	0	3	X	5
Brooklyn	0	1	0	0	0	1	2	0	0	4

Summary

Two-base hits—Delan, Daly. Three-base hits—Davis. Sacrifice hits—Phillippi, Irwin. Stolen bases—Beaumont, Wagner, Kelley. Double plays—Burke to Bransfield, Dahlen to Kelley, Daley to Dahlen to Kelley. Bases on balls—Off Kitson, 2. Struck out—by Phillippi, 2; by Kitson, 2. Time of game—1 hr. 55 m. Umpire—Emillo. Attendance 3500.

Now, don't those names bring back memories to you old fans?

The Brooklyn club was a mighty strong outfit then and this game put them out of the running. They had previously been the champions.

We beat Brooklyn out by simply running away with the game. We had the greatest base-running outfit I ever saw. Our system was to take an extra base on every hit when there was even half a chance. We ran bases all the time and if a runner got on first you could be sure he was going to pull something. As a result we had the other clubs up in the air.

Six Shut-Outs in a Row

That same team, which won the pennant again in 1903 as well as 1902, established a world's record for shut-outs. We shut out our opponents six times in succession. I happen to have the record in my scrap book. Look:

> June 2—Pittsburgh 7, New York 0, pitchers Leever vs. McGinnity
> June 3—Pittsburgh 5, New York 0, pitchers Wilhelm vs. Platt
> June 4—Pittsburgh 5, Boston, 0, pitchers Doheny vs. Pittenger
> June 5—Pittsburgh 9, Boston 0, pitchers Phillips vs. Willis
> June 6—Pittsburgh 4, Boston 0, pitchers Leever vs. Sparks
> June 7—Pittsburgh 3, Philadelphia 0, pitchers Phillips vs. —

We were on the way to a seventh shut-out in the next game; it went to the seventh inning, when Roy Thomas scored on an outfield . . . [sic].

Now, if that wasn't a great ball club, I'd like to see one. No other club ever had pitchers work like that or ever made any such record.

Mind you, we had lost some of our best men when we did that. In 1902 several players went to the American League and made great records there. Among them was Harry Smith, a great catcher, one of the best in the world at holding runners on base.

Another great man we lost was Jack Chesbro, who went to the New York Americans, then just starting, and made a wonderful record. Chesbro was called Happy Jack, and rightly so. He had a wonderful disposition and was always ready to pitch. He had wonderful speed with a jump on his fast ball. Later he picked up the spitball and got famous with it. He is supposed to be the first pitcher to develop the spitball perfectly.

LIGHTEST BALL

There were some men on that team who made my grand all-American team and several others who came pretty near it. Take Tommy Leach, for instance. There was a great third baseman, despite his small stature. Then Claude Ritchey was at second. He was the best man I ever saw in picking up ground balls between the bounces. Nothing seemed to fool him. Claude was never a great hitter except in a pinch. But then is when you could bet on him. That is why the fans gave him the name of Little All-Right.

Chief Zimmer was also on that team, leaving in 1902. The Chief threw the lightest ball to second I ever handled. You could catch it without a glove. The man who is not a baseball player probably does not know that some players throw what is known as a heavy ball. It drops in the glove like a ton of lead. Others throw one as light as a feather. Just why that is I don't know and I never knew anybody else that knew. There have been some third basemen and shortstops who threw such a heavy ball to first that the baseman could hardly hold it.

The other stars were Schoolmaster Leever, Deacon Phillippi, Ed Doheny, Jesse Tannehill and Bill Kennedy, pitchers; Jimmy Webring, Ed Phelps (he caught every game in the 1903 world's series); Jimmy Williams, infielder (went to the American League in 1903); Jack O'Connor, Kitty Barnsfield and others. We had another great player named Davis, who did not last long because he broke a leg.

Yes, I'd like to go on record as saying that's the best ball club I ever saw.

The All-Star National League Team for Thirty Years

• • •

After going over them all, studying their hitting and fielding ability, their aggressiveness, love of the game and teamwork, here is my selection for the all-star National League team of the past thirty years:

Manager—Fred Clarke
Captain—Hughey Jennings
First Base—Jake Daubert
Second Base—Napoleon Lajoie
Shortstop—Hughey Jennings
Third Base—Jimmy Collins
Left Field—Fred Clarke
Center Field—Jesse Burkett
Right Field—Willie Keeler
Extra Outfielder—Joe Kelley
Extra Infielder—Rogers
    Hornsby
Catchers—Johnny Kling, Roger
    Bresnahan, George Gibson
Pitchers—Christy Mathewson,
    Mordecai Brown, Grover
    Cleveland Alexander, Deacon
    Phillipi, Babe Adams

The players I have given here were masters of every trick in the game, fair and unfair. They knew how to make them and how to break them up. I don't know of anything that could be put over on these boys.

I have considered the question of right- and left-handed hitters. I also realize that my club is short of left-handed pitchers, but with that outfit I wouldn't need southpaws.

Jake Daubert, Fred Clarke, Jesse Burkett and Willie Keeler could hit left-handed pitching just as well as right-handed pitching. I would certainly feel sorry for any pitcher who had to face such a ball club with the lively ball now in use. The hit-and-run play would be pie for those birds. The lively ball would rarely ever get stopped in the infield. They would run the bases almost as they pleased.

Before anybody starts in to criticize my selection, I wish they would sit down and compare the brains of those players with others they have in mind. Every one of them was noted for aggressiveness and a desire to win that kept them fighting until the last man was out in the ninth.

EVERY MAN A MASTER

Every man on that club was a master in his position. A manager would have a soft job. You would seldom hear anybody ask "Who won?" It would be "What's the score?"

The length of service, to my way of thinking, must always be considered in selecting a ball club. That counts extra big because it enables a team to keep on winning pennants without making changes.

I picked Hornsby as my extra infielder not because everybody else picked him, but for a definite purpose. Aside from his heavy hitting, he can play any position in the infield and could go in at any minute as a pinch-hitter. The same thing goes for Joe Kelley in the outfield. It's pretty hard to leave Joe off of any regular all-star team. He was a marvelous outfielder, a great thrower, a sure hitter and a fighting Irishman.

Roger Bresnahan also could be used anywhere on the club. He has played every position, having started out as a pitcher and finished as a catcher.

Each one of those players knows how to get in condition and keep in condition. They would train to be in perfect shape, not because it was the rule, but because they would know what was best for them. We would seldom need the utility men.

I have not named a big pitching staff. Those I have selected would be ample. All of them would be better off with a lot of work to do.

Some of these players, you will notice, are also on my all-American team for all time. Let us consider the others:

George Gibson, as a third catcher, was a fair hitter and an iron man for work. He was a good man for pitchers. They all liked to work with him. When a team was in a rut, I never knew a better man for getting it out than Gibson. He knew the weakness of every hitter in the league and was clever at outguessing base runners. Another big thing in his favor was the way he got along with the umpires. The catcher, you know, can save many a bad situation by talking quietly with the umpire who stands near him. Wilbert Robinson was also great at that.

MINER BROWN'S CURVE

Miner Brown* is one pitcher I'd certainly have to use. He knew all the tricks of the trade. He had terrific speed for a man his size and had a big, quick breaking outcurve that was a puzzler. That old curve, I believe, was due to his having but three fingers. The curve was different from that of anybody else. He was a wonderful fielder also, and a good hitter and base runner. Brown was very tricky and kept his opponents guessing all the time. He was willing to pitch any time and particularly liked to be stacked against the star pitcher of the opposition. He was very aggressive. It was Miner Brown who was called to the rescue and saved that play-off game between the Giants and Cubs for the pennant in 1908.

Charles (Deacon) Phillippi was another great pitcher who always wanted to be sent in against the star of the opposing game. He reveled in a hard fight. His greatest quality was that he never in his life complained about errors being made back of him. He took it all as part of the game. He was ready to pitch in any kind of weather and was always anxious to be selected. Phillippi had everything that a pitcher ought to have and he used the Mathewson system of pitching to his fielders. That is, he would figure to make a batter hit in a certain direction and let the outfield do the big share of the work until he got into a tight pinch. He was a star in the world's series between the Pirates and the Boston Red Sox.

Babe Adams was the best pitcher I ever saw to bring his club out of a losing rut. He had terrific speed, a jump on his fast one, good curves—everything. There is no doubt about Adams being one of the greatest pitchers in the world. He won three games in the world's

• • •

*Better known today as Mordecai, or "Three Finger," Brown (1876–1948). He pitched shutouts in the 1906, 1907 and 1908 World Series. Only Whitey Ford has pitched as many World Series shutouts.

series between Pittsburgh and Detroit, shutting them out, 8 to 0, in the deciding game.

HE NEVER GOT HIS DUE

Jake Daubert, my first baseman, is a better man than he ever got credit for being. He is a wonder on shifting his feet when forced to catch wild throws. Handling the feet is more important in a first baseman than his hands. Most anybody can catch the ball. The feet must put him in position to do so and also to get him out of the way of the base runner. Jake is very good on low throws.

Hughey Jennings was one of the smartest shortstops that ever lived. He was always inventing new plays and was the first short-stop to take a throw from the catcher and tag the base runner while on the run. At the bat he was a good hitter and was very smart in getting on base by being hit with a pitched ball if it was necessary. Hughey was a wonderful fielder and a great student of the game.

Jesse Burkett was a great hitter, fielder and base runner. He was the greatest in control of bunting when the catcher used to play back. Jesse would make the ball stop not more than a foot in front of the plate. He was so tricky at this that all the catchers in the league had to take every ball off the bat when he was up. Burkett liked to play; lived and talked baseball.

There is no use for me to speak of Willie Keeler. He has been on nearly every all-American and all-National team ever picked. He was simply a little wizard. Poor little Keeler is gone now. I take my hat off to him. There was never another like him. He invented most of the batting and outfield tricks that other ball players are still trying to learn.

Famous Fans in
Baseball History

• • •

In picking out some of the famous fans of my time, I will start by naming the president of our club, Barney Dreyfuss. He was the only club owner I ever knew who was just as rabid a fan as any rooter in the grandstand. He got in the game first as a fan and not merely to start a new business, as a lot of people think.

So much has been said of Barney Dreyfuss as a wise baseball owner, a smart trader and a man who understands every angle of the baseball business that few know of him as a fan. Barney has calmed down in his later days and can take the games as they come without getting excited.

If you ever sat next to him in a grandstand in the old days, though, and didn't know him by sight, you'd never think the rooter next to you was the owner of the Pittsburgh club. His comments would run something like this:

"Oh, there's a hit! . . . I knew it when Johnny gave him a low ball. He couldn't hit a high one with a shovel! . . . Huh, there he goes again—walking Jones, a weak hitter, so as to get at Smith who's been slamming the ball hard all season. Huh! That's fine judgment, I don't think!"

Then a ground ball would go for a clean base hit between third and short.

"What's that shortstop playing near second for on a dead left-field hitter? Well, that's fine! What's Johnny watching that runner for—he's an ice wagon on the bases. Sure. He can't run the length of a base without stopping. G'on, pitch to the batter, never mind the base runner!"

With Barney's own club at bat he would go like this:

"Scoops ought to bunt—look, that third baseman is playing back a mile." The batter does bunt and beats it. "That's the

150

boy, that's playing the game. Now, there's a chance for sacrifice." Batter bunts a pop fly that is caught. "Huh, bunts like a drunken shoemaker—picking on a high ball to bunt—bound to pop it in the air."

Next two batters go out on long flies.

"No runs, huh! Bum ball playing!"

HE KNOWS EVERY HOPEFUL

Mr. Dreyfuss would travel with the team, mix up with the players and engage in any of their games, their amusements. He would mix up in practical jokes and give and take. But, above all things, he was crazy to see his ball club win.

I remember once we were defeated by the Giants in a remarkable game that went eighteen innings, the Pirates being defeated in the last inning, 2 to 0.

"That was certainly a nice game of ball," I remarked to him when we got to the hotel, "and a great crowd present, too."

"Huh," he grunted, "but don't forget, Honus, that we lost the ball game."

Barney Dreyfuss probably knows more baseball than any owner in the game. There are no plays or players with which he is not at all familiar. He has made the study of ball players all over the country a science. You couldn't stump him to this day on any ball player in the country, major or minor league. When it comes to a system of knowing what is going on in connection with baseball, he could make a Scotland Yard detective look like a busher.

Mr. Dreyfuss gets a line on youngsters even before they enter high schools, also young players so far back in the woods that they only come out but once in a year. I found this out while hunting in the different backwoods of the country. Old farmers and woodsmen would mention Barney Dreyfuss having had a scout out there on certain ball players. He keeps a line on the way they are developing year after year. When they are ripe he either gets them or marks them off his little dope book. Once he runs that mark through a youngster's name you can bet that young fellow will never make the big league. Barney never makes a mistake on them. He has a wonderful mem-

Honus Wagner was an avid hunter in the off-season. He is kneeling in the foreground, surrounded by his four favorite dogs, in this picture. His brother Al is at the extreme right. *(Baseball Magazine)*

ory and knows the good and bad points of young players whether he ever has seen them or not. Just mention any young fellow to him and you'll find that Mr. Dreyfuss knows lots more about his playing than you do. He can even tell you the boy's personal habits.

WHERE HE GOT THEM

Barney Dreyfuss is a hard worker. All he asks of a player is to give him his best and obey the club rules. It is his belief that a ball player owes it to the public to give the fans a run for their money. If they deliver the goods they can depend upon Barney remembering them for their efforts.

Mr. Dreyfuss has been more successful in developing youngsters than in paying high prices for men who never have and never will win their spurs. For instance, here are some great stars that he dug

Robert "Ham" Hyatt was a North Carolina native who debuted with Pittsburgh in 1909. He played first base and outfield, but was mostly used as a
pinch hitter. In 1913, he pinch-hit in 53 games, fielded in only 10 games,
but hit .333 in 81 at-bats, with an on-base percentage (OBP) of .372 and a
slugging percentage of .605. (George Brace Photo Collection)

out of the backwoods—men who knew nothing about cities or big leagues: Deacon Phillippi, Redfield, South Dakota; Sam Leever, Goshen, Ohio; Jack Chesbro, Massachusetts; Brickyard Bill Kennedy, Martin's Ferry, Ohio; Rube Waddell, Biano, Pennsylvania; Clarence Beaumont, Honey Creek, Wisconsin; Babe Adams, Mt. Moriah, Missouri; Ham Hyatt, Northwoods, and I might say myself from Mansfield, Pennsylvania. It's a cinch I didn't know much when they grabbed me and put me in a league uniform.

I could name fifty towns that you never heard of in the rural districts that furnished players to Barney Dreyfuss.

Dreyfuss has a good sense of humor and used to get many laughs out of the funny cracks made by the ball players. One time when we were in New York and having a very disastrous trip we crossed over to some town in New Jersey on a ferry. Just as we landed and started for the ball yards for an exhibition game we noticed a signboard, to direct traffic which read:

"Slow Moving Teams This Way—."

We all stopped and looked, almost afraid to laugh.

"Looks like they got us right," some young players remarked, and Mr. Dreyfuss had his first good laugh for a week.

On that same trip we had felt that we were getting the worst of a lot of things, umpires' decisions included. It seemed like the umpires actually took a delight in calling our men out. I guess they didn't, but we felt so badly about our slump that it actually did look like the umpires made a special effort to show off when one of our men struck out or was waved out at the plate.

On our ferry boat we went close to the Statue of Liberty, which many of the players had never seen before. You know, a lot of folks come to New York all their lives and never see the Statue of Liberty.

"What does she remind you of?" I asked Fred Clarke, as we looked up at the great figure of a woman, holding her hand high and rigid, with a torch in it.

"Looks like Bill Klem calling a third strike," he said.

To this day, that is the way I always picture the Statue of Liberty in my mind.

Some of the well-known fans of that day—we don't have them like we used to, it seems—were Barney McKenna, a Pittsburgh Police

Magistrate; W. H. Eaton of Oil City, Penn.; Honey Boy Evans,* the famous minstrel who donated the annual loving cup to the champion batter of both leagues, which I now have in my trophy room, incidentally; De Wolf Hopper,† the actor; Johnny Harris of Crafton, Penn.; and Lew Wentz of Pittsburgh.§ I have mentioned but a few.

These fans, mind you, use to leave their business and take trips with the teams they rooted for. They never missed a game at home and if the race got close, they would take to the road.

Nowadays some players seem to look upon the wild-eyed fans who follow the teams around as sort of pests. That's all wrong. These are the fellows who made the game, who made our big salaries possible.

In my next chapter I will present my selection of an all-American League team.

• • •

*George "Honey Boy" Evans (1870–1915), originally from Wales, was a composer and black-faced minstrel, the most famous of this time. He wrote the ever-popular song, "In the Good Old Summertime," first performed by his wife, the vaudeville singer Blanche Ring, and later performed by Judy Garland and by Stan Laurel and Oliver Hardy.

†De Wolf Hopper (1858–1935), U.S. actor and comedian. Born William De Wolf Hopper in New York City. He is best remembered for his recitations of Ernest Thayer's poem "Casey at the Bat" and for starring in Gilbert and Sullivan's comic operas, including *The Mikado, Patience,* and *H.M.S. Pinafore.* He was married to gossip columnist Hedda Hopper.

§Louis Haines Wentz (1877–1949). Lew Wentz, the son of a blacksmith, was raised with six brothers and sisters in Pittsburgh. He loved children, Shetland ponies, the Republican Party and baseball: playing, organizing teams, and coaching. Never married and too poor for college as a young man, Wentz was coaching high school ball and campaigning door to door for the GOP when he met a wealthy man who offered him a chance to join in an oil venture in Oklahoma. In 1911, Wentz moved there and by 1927 was "the world's richest bachelor." In 1926, he established foundations for student loans at four Oklahoma colleges, each receiving $50,000. When Wentz sold his oil interests just before the stock market crash of 1929, he increased his support for higher education, donating a number of Texas oil leases to his foundation. He attempted to buy the St. Louis Cardinals in 1934. Today, the Wentz Foundations provide several million dollars annually to Oklahoma college students.

An All-American
League Team

• • •

Here is what, in my opinion, would make the best team of American League players since that league was organized:

Manager—Tris Speaker
Captain—Ty Cobb
First Base—George Sisler
Second Base—Eddie Collins
Third Base—Jimmy Collins
Shortstop—Fred Parent
Extra Infielder—Roy Chapman
Left Field—Ty Cobb
Center Field—Tris Speaker
Right Field—Babe Ruth
Extra Outfielder—Sam
 Crawford
Catchers—Ray Schalk, Billy
 Sullivan, Lou Criger
Pitchers—Ed Walsh, Cy Denton
 Young, Walter Johnson, Red
 Faber and Rube Waddell

I realize that my club is somewhat different from those selected by other old-timers but, if such a thing were possible, I would like mighty well to stack mine against any I have seen and bet a hat on the result.

I have not stuck to the records, but have picked men who could play ball when counted on. To tell the truth I think club spirit and general aggressiveness count a lot more than figures in getting together a ball club to win.

Naturally the manager and captain on this club would have a soft job, but you will notice that I have saved a lot of money for the management by having both my manager and captain as players in the regular line-up. I always liked a playing manager, anyway.

Now, there is a ball club to which the fine points of the game are second nature. All a manager would have to do would be to lay out a system. He could depend on every one of them knowing what he was talking about and working it out to the best advantage.

HOW SAFE WOULD YOU FEEL?

I have selected a team of wonderful hitters, base runners and fielders. Also I have considered the throwing arms. That is mighty important.

The way that team could field, though, they wouldn't need to be such terrible hitters. With that kind of a pitching staff behind them a couple of runs would look as big as an ordinary dozen.

How safe would you feel if you had a two-run lead with Rube Waddell or Walter Johnson pitching? The same thing goes for Young, Walsh and Faber. What do you suppose John McGraw, or any other manager, would give for a pitching staff like that today?

Many of these players have been placed on my grand all-American team of all time and have been fully discussed—notably, by Cy Young, Walter Johnson, Jimmy Collins, Eddie Collins, Babe Ruth, Tris Speaker, Ty Cobb, Rube Waddell and George Sisler. Maybe you are not familiar with some of the others. Incidentally, it is interesting to me to notice how nearly even the two leagues are in furnishing stars to the Grand All-American team. Of course, several of them played in both leagues.

Ed Walsh, to my mind, was one of the game's greatest pitchers. He had wonderful control and terrific speed. When his speed fell off a little he suddenly turned to the spitball and was a whirlwind with it. He had the brains to take advantage of every new wrinkle and studied his business closely. Walsh had good curves and a remarkable change of pace. He could stand a lot of work and was always willing to go in. He was also a good hitter and fielder.

Urban (Red) Faber is another great pitcher who has been overlooked sometimes in picking ball clubs. He was particularly good on locating the weakness of opposing batters. He had a big assortment of curves and mixed them up well. Faber went around the world as an extra pitcher with the Giants, though he really belonged to the White Sox. There's an odd story about that. Mr. Comiskey had sent him back to Des Moines, but when the Giants and White Sox were short of pitchers for the trip, it was decided to take Faber along as a sort of helper-out. After seeing him work a few times McGraw told Comiskey that he had rather have Faber than any man on the White Sox staff.

THEY CALLED HIM BACK

"If you mean that, John, I'll recall him from Des Moines and give him another chance next season."

He did that and Faber turned out to be Chicago's great winning pitcher in capturing the American League pennant.

Sam Crawford came pretty close to getting on my Grand All-American team. He certainly belongs on the all-American League outfit. There was a boy who could crash the old apple. Not only could he hit but he could field. Crawford was the best of them all in handling ground balls in the outfield. It was mighty hard to take an extra base on him. I always thought that Crawford would have made a marvelous first baseman. He is now running a school for ball players and is turning out some mighty good prospects.

Fred Parent is another grand ball player, who never got all the credit he deserved for some reason. He was a graceful player who made hard plays look easy. I think Parent the greatest shortstop I ever saw in starting and finishing double plays and also at breaking up the double steal. Fred simply loved to play ball. He was a good hitter and base runner as well as a fielder. He had a great throwing arm and could peg the ball from any position as accurate as a rifle shot. Parent was especially good at tagging base runners when they slid.

Ray Chapman, who was accidentally killed when hit by a pitched ball, would undoubtedly have made one of the greatest ball players the game ever knew had he lived longer. There is no play known to the game that he couldn't make well. He was a good hitter and a very smart base runner. It was worth a lot to the Cleveland team to get him on base. Ray would always start some kind of a rally. No infielder was better than Chapman on tagging out a base runner. Those who have not played big league ball may not realize how difficult a trick that is—touching a sliding runner with the ball and then getting out of the way of his spikes. It must be done in a skillful manner so that the umpire can see clearly that the runner is out. The umpire often will miss a clumsy or awkward tag of the runner. Chapman had no fear at all. He was extremely aggressive and very confident. It is too bad that he had to pass away as he did. All ball players loved Ray.

Billy Sullivan was one of the very great old-time catchers. He was a wonderful man to pitch to, always keeping the pitchers cool and deliberate. In fact nobody ever got excited with Sullivan behind the bat. He seemed to keep the whole club on an even balance.

Sullivan always gave the infield confidence by calling the plays for them to make. He also was sure that they got the pitching signs. Billy could hit, field and run bases, and was never bothered by any kind of pitching. In other words, Billy Sullivan was a great catcher.

Lou Criger was another old star that I would want on my ball club. He liked the game and knew every fine point. He was cool and deliberate and had an arm like a whip. I think Criger was as good a catcher as I ever saw on breaking up the double steal. He seemed to have a knack of knowing when the runner would start and whether the man on third was really coming in or was merely making a bluff of it. He picked off many a one of them. Criger was a good hitter and base runner.

Yes, I think that would be a winning all-American League team. No doubt of it.

The Most Spectacular Catch Ever Seen

• • •

The most spectacular catch ever seen in baseball, in my opinion, was made by Jack Murray, outfielder of the Giants, at a game in Pittsburgh. This is probably the only play ever made that was aided by a flash of lightning.

As some of you may know, heavy rain clouds and the smoke from the various industrial plants and factories occasionally make it dark in Pittsburgh long before the hour of sunset. On those days the ball games are very gloomy affairs. I have known of a game being called on account of darkness long before 4 o'clock.

On this particular day the Giants and Pirates were in a tie in a hard-fought game. Finally the Giants got a lead just as it grew so dark that it was almost impossible to see the outfielders. A dark, black cloud came up and behind it we knew a storm was coming. We tried to hurry the game along as we had men on bases and a chance to win.

While the batter was waiting on the pitcher, lightning flashes showed through the cloud, followed by heavy thunder, and the crowd in the bleachers started for shelter.

The storm burst just as the batter swung on the ball. He hit it squarely on the nose. Everybody could hear the crack, but in the growing darkness we could not see the ball. In fact, we could barely make out the form of the outfielder. Just at that moment, though, there was a great flash of lightning. It lighted up the field as a flash at night would do. In the flash we saw Jack Murray going for the ball. He also saw the ball by the flash and with a leap reached it. From where we sat it was plain to see that he had speared the ball, but in a fraction of a second the whole ground was almost dark. Just the same Murray came dashing in with the ball and the umpire called the batter out.

That catch made by the aid of a flash of lightning had put our side out and won the game. There was no question about the catch being fair.

In all my experience, that was the most spectacular finish to a ball game that I ever hope to see.

OUTFIELD LOST IN MIST

There have been several odd cases like that but none so exciting as Murray's catch. In Chicago only a year ago a mist blew in over the field from the lake and was so thick that the outfielders could not be seen. The Giants and Cubs were playing. McGraw has told me that that was the only game he ever took part in when he couldn't see his outfielders, sometimes for two innings. The game having started under those conditions the umpires refused to stop. Pop Young tells me that he was in right field when he heard a ball whistling by his ear. A few minutes later one came to him on the first bounce and he tried to make it appear that he had caught it on the fly. Luckily for the Cubs one of the umpires ran through the fog after the ball and claims he saw Young trap it. Young never denied it.

In one game out at Exposition Park, the old Pittsburgh grounds which backed up on the river, Clarence Beaumont was playing centerfield. He backed up so far that he was knee deep in water in attempting to catch a fly. He made the catch for the last out, but in doing so stumbled and fell, going completely out of sight beneath the water.

In a game between Louisville and Cleveland, Dummy Hoy was the victim of the funniest accident I think I ever saw. He had backed up as far as he could go when he tripped and fell, the ball coming down and hitting him squarely on the head as he lay on the ground.

"Looks like we'll have to give our outfielders masks from now on or they'll get their brains knocked out," Fred Clarke remarked when the laugh had died down.

Jake Beckley, a very tricky player in the old days, got caught at one of his own tricks one day in a way that gave us a big laugh. Jake had a way of hiding the ball under his arm at first base so as to catch the runner when he wandered off.

DIDN'T COME OFF

The batter this day had got a two-base hit and was on second. Beckley took the ball from the outfield and promptly hid it under his arm. He gave the pitcher the sign to go ahead and pretend to pitch.

With everything set the runner made a break to go from second to third sooner than Jake had expected. There was a great lot of yelling and laughter from Jake's teammates but something happened and he couldn't get the ball out from under his arm until the runner was perched on third base. Jake then disgustedly rolled the ball to the pitcher.

Beckley, by the way, was one of the first base runners to use the old trick of cutting across the diamond from second base to the plate without going to third. In the days when we had but one umpire a runner often could get away with that because the umpire would be watching the batter or the ball.

One day Jake cut the bases and was caught at it. Notwithstanding that he had been caught red handed, he actually raised a big holler of protest over the decision.

Many funny things happen on the ball field that do not seem so funny when written on paper. I think a man must see them to appreciate how ridiculous they are. For instance, Leo King got into an argument with Chief Meyers, the catcher, one day and started punching at the Indian who had on his mask, his chest protector and his shin guards. Now there is what I call a man taking the worst of it. Chief Meyers got to laughing so that he couldn't fight back. Even the umpire got to laughing and let King go on and play without punishment.

At Forbes Field one afternoon pitcher Fred Toney was put out of the game by the umpire. He walked over to the bench and picked up a pick and shovel, left there by the groundkeeper. Very seriously he walked straight across the diamond with the tools on his shoulder.

We were playing a game at Boston with Bill Klem umpiring, and as the score was going against us we all started riding Klem by yelping at him from the bench.

"Why don't you call one right some time," one of our recruits yelled at Klem, "just to see how it feels?"

AND ALL HAD TO SNORE

That was the straw that broke the camel's back. Klem, taking off his mask, walked right over to our bench to see just who it was that had been doing so much kicking of his decision—who were making wise cracks.

We all immediately pulled our caps down over our eyes, rested our chins on our chests and started snoring, pretending that we were asleep.

"Sleep, are you?" he snapped at us in that biting voice of his. "All right, stay asleep then. The first man on that bench who wakes up will get put out of the game. That goes, too."

We knew Klem well enough to know that he would do just what he said. Our club had just got a one-run lead and for fear of having some of our best players put off we had to sit there and pretend to be asleep for the next two innings. Not a soul of us dared look up, except when called to bat.

That's one time an umpire put it over on us.

When I was a young player, I was a little timid about talking to umpires, simply because I couldn't think of anything to say, as a rule. Fred Clarke reminded me the other day of a run-in I had with Tim Hurst.

There had been a close play at third base, where I was playing that day. Everybody ran in to make a kick and I decided to take a hand also. I ran up to Hurst and was about to open my mouth when—

"What are you doing here?" he demanded. "Are you the captain of this team?"

"No, sir," I said, sort of taken back, "but I'm captain of third base."

Hurst was good-natured enough to let me off with that.

All's Fair in Love and Baseball

• • •

A few people who have just a fair working knowledge of baseball seem to be confused over the words crookedness and trickiness as applied to the game. They have asked me to relate any crooked incident that I ever saw. The answer is that I never saw one. If a player were actually crooked in baseball, there is hardly a player who wouldn't help to get him blacklisted for life immediately.

The word crookedness, when applied to baseball, is often mixed up with what some folks call lack of sportsmanship. As I have said before, we never thought much about what was sportsmanship and what wasn't in the old days. We used every trick that we could think of to win.

A crooked player is one who will use tricks to lose. See the difference?

In all my life I have never heard of but two cases of down-right crookedness, actual dishonesty. That was in the case of the players of the White Sox who were put out on a charge of having sold out to some gamblers, their agreement being to let the Reds win the first two games. Many years before, long before my time even, three other players were thrown out and disgraced for throwing games.

It is mighty hard for a ball player to throw a game even if he wants to. It would be impossible for one man to do it. The minute he seemed to be going badly, the manager would take him out. It requires several in a conspiracy to actually throw a game. For instance, a shortstop might decide to be crooked in a game and not a single ball would be hit to him all day.

In the first place, a ball player is a fool to be crooked because he cannot possibly gain anything by it in the long run. There is no incentive. He can make more money by winning than by losing. If he should get a sum of money for throwing a game he would lose many times that amount by being blacklisted for life out of the game.

The real secret of baseball's success as a sport is that it must be honest. Nowhere in the world does honesty pay better than in baseball. The clubs who win the most games, you know, draw the biggest patronage. The loss of patronage would overcome any possible gain they might make by selling out. The same thing goes for the players. Those on a winning team get increases in salary. In other words, every incentive in the game is to win.

PUTTING IT OVER IS DIFFERENT

Besides, there wouldn't be any fun or any thrill in baseball if it could be juggled around like some other event. With us it is a life work and an everyday thing. While a wrestler or a boxer has one night every three or four months, a ball player must be on his job every day of the week. No man can be happy and be dishonest.

Baseball players are essentially a happy lot.

But when it comes to trickery, schemes to beat the other fellow out, that is different. There is a sort of feeling among ball players, despite what you may have read, that anything is fair that they can get away with. Anyway, that was the idea in the old days.

I remember one day when Al Mamaux first started pitching in the big league; the Pirates and Giants were playing. Mamaux had been going pretty well until some Giant hit a two-base hit with a man on first. This put runners on second and third. There was a conference between Mamaux and some of our players around the pitcher's box. Roger Bresnahan was on the coaching line for the Giants.

"Hey," he yelled to Mamaux just as the conference broke up, "let me see that ball."

Mamaux, being a youngster and thinking that Bresnahan wanted to see if anything was wrong with the ball, tossed it to him. Bresnahan promptly jumped out of the way and let the ball roll to the stand. Both runners scored. You can imagine what a razzing Mamaux got!

Now that may have been unsportsmanlike but it was looked upon as a pretty good joke. Bresnahan had simply got away with an old trick, as old as hiding the ball.

If a man gets away with a trick like that in baseball, the big league players never complain, but there is an unwritten law that a player must not purposely injure another. More trouble is caused over that among ball players than any one thing. Most of the time these injuries are accidental, but in the heart of the game it is perfectly natural for a player to complain that a base-runner deliberately cut into him with his spikes.

RUBE WADDELL SHOWED HE COULD

Injuring a man naturally puts him out of business and may stop his only method of making a living. Therefore, to deliberately hurt a man is considered a very mean act.

One time at the Polo Grounds McGraw, knowing that Rube Waddell was to pitch against the Giants, nagged him into a throwing contest before the game. He had Waddell throwing his arm off to see who could make the longest peg to the plate. Rube got so interested and tired that when it came to the game he was so weak he couldn't pitch at all. In the old days that was considered strategy and nobody ever thought of criticizing McGraw. The other manager simply gave Waddell the dickens of a call down for being a sucker.

Another old tire-'em-out trick that sometimes worked with young pitchers was to catch them in a chase between the bases. The opposing infielders would throw the ball back and forward until the poor pitcher had run his tongue out. They never had any intention of catching him. They just kept throwing the ball to make him run up and down the base line. That is also a favorite old trick to play on recruits in the spring training camps.

Fred Clarke once played a trick on one of McGraw's young pitchers that the Giant manager has never forgotten. This young fellow prided himself on his control.

"Hey, you've got no control," Clarke called to him. "I'll bet you $2 you can't throw a ball behind the batter." This was said so that nobody else could hear it.

Sure enough, the angry young fellow did throw one behind the batter that went wild, allowing two men to score and losing the game for McGraw.

The funniest part of that to me was that the young pitcher came around that night looking for Clarke so as to collect his $2 bet.

Chuckles and Chores in Spring Training

• • •

Spring training always has been to me a sort of lark, and I think it is to most of the regulars who know how to prepare themselves and have no particular worry about their jobs. During the off hours they can sit back and have all the laughs.

For some men, though, spring training is very hard work. When the day is over they are quite ready to crawl in bed at nine o'clock and nurse their sore muscles and bruises. There are some ball players, by the way, who never have had muscular soreness in the spring. Just why that is I do not know, unless it is that they have kept up their athletic exercises during the winter. Personally I never had any trouble at all in getting in shape. To tell the truth, the spring training was much easier to me than the hunting, basketball, indoor baseball and so on that I did during the winter.

Always there has been an open discussion as to the advantages of a long training trip or a short one. Some managers even contend that it is better to train pretty well north so that the players will not be affected by the sudden change in climate as they come back home. Clarke Griffith tried this scheme with good results in Virginia. The great majority, though, find it better to go far south where the players, due to the warmth, can ease up their tired muscles without catching cold.

The Pittsburgh club has found Hot Springs to be the best training place. I always liked it there. Walking up and down those Arkansas mountains was a good muscle builder in itself. You can't walk anywhere in Hot Springs without going up or down hill. The hot waters help a lot in loosening up the muscles.

The main thing the pitchers

have to acquire is control. They work in gradually, getting stronger and more accurate day by day.

McGraw Has Rigid Rules

The main point in spring training, according to my observation, is the chance of trying out the recruits and seeing what they really can do. Some managers allow the old-timers to get in shape according to their own ideas. Others have a rigid system and even the most famous and experienced players have to follow the discipline. The idea of this is that it sets an example for the youngsters. John McGraw is one of those who has a rigid system. One thing about him, though—he will do everything he asks the youngest player to do. He is the first man up in the morning and the last one to leave the field at night.

Miller Huggins, of the champion Yankees, used the system last year of letting the seasoned players get in shape as they deemed best. That worked out all right, too. They won the pennant and the world's championship. So you never can tell which is best. I think the biggest result, after all, is that the players get to know each other better and establish themselves as sort of a family before the hard season starts.

There is never any particular what a player should eat. It must be remembered that a ball player is different from all other athletes in that he has to prepare for an everyday job that lasts all summer. Therefore he must live just as naturally as possible. There is little difference between the diet of a ball player and of any ordinary business man.

To me it was always the fun, the practical jokes and the skylarking of a southern training trip that appealed. I like to laugh, even though I was never much of a jokester myself.

One of the old gags that always gave me a laugh was on the train going to the camp. There would be a lot of raw, young recruits who, of course, had to take upper berths. Rank is as strict in baseball as in the army. The regulars must have the lower berths and they look on it as a matter of right. In fact, the privilege of a lower berth sort of marks a fellow as having made good. For a young recruit to take a lower would be considered a terrible affront to the veterans. It would be like treason.

THE TEXAN GOT THE THIEF!

Well, when those young fellows start most of them have never ridden in a Pullman sleeper and don't really know the difference between an upper and lower. They learn quick, though. We used to tell the youngsters as they were climbing into their uppers that they had better give all their small change to the porters to keep for them as it might fall out of their pockets.

Wanting to do the right thing these poor young kids would shell out their small change to the porter, who would thank them. The next morning they would get such a laugh that they would never even think of asking for it again.

That was a cruel trick to play on these kids, who rarely ever had any more change than the law allows, but it was funny, at that.

We had one big awkward fellow get on the train going to Hot Springs and we called him Red right off the reel. He watched the poker games for awhile, tried to talk baseball to Mr. Clarke—did everything to make himself agreeable.

"Now," one of the boys told him, "coming as a young fellow you had better sit up tonight and guard the valuables. Anything is likely to happen on a train like this. That young fellow over there will be on guard duty tomorrow night."

"Sure," agreed Red. "Glad to do it. I'll watch everything."

He was a big Texan and the look in his eye showed that he meant to do that duty properly, too.

During the night the young fellow, who was half dozing, woke up to see a man going out the door with a whole armful of shoes. He got on the job immediately.

I was awakened to hear a terrible commotion up in the smoking compartment. I heard my name called several times,

"Come up here and help me, Mr. Wagner," he called out. "I've got him, all right."

I went up there and had to wait until the door was unlocked. Then I found the porter over in the corner, scared to death and the big Texan standing over him holding a pistol.

He had chased that porter down, had taken away the shoes that he was shining and had locked him up in the smoking compartment until he got help.

WHAT THOSE NETS ARE FOR

Every ball club in the world, I suppose, works the old gag of making the youngsters sleep with their arms in the little hammocks, so as to keep from falling out of their berths and also to protect their pitching arms.

Claude Ritchey once made a left-handed pitcher move so as to get on the side which had left-handed hammocks.

In this 1930s photo, Honus Wagner demonstrates the batting stance with which he hit above .299 for the first 16 years of his 21-year career. In this pose, he is not using the split-grip. (George Brace Photo Collection)

What to Look for
in a Game

● ● ●

When I began this narrative of baseball as I have seen and studied it, I had no idea that so many business and professional men would be interested in what you might call the technique of the play. I have received almost as many requests from elderly fans as from amateur players and young professionals for my views on the fine points of the game.

I will, therefore, devote my concluding articles to a sort of final examination in the hope that it will help build up young teams as well as give the spectators a clearer appreciation of what the ball players are trying to do on the field. Many of these questions are taken from the examination papers I prepared for the boys at Carnegie Tech, where I was coach.

In previous articles I have suggested questions on the defensive side of baseball. These will be on the offensive side, the side that I like.

STRAIGHTAWAY HITTING

1. Do you always play the waiting style of game at the beginning?
2. Is it good policy to hit the first ball now and then?
3. Is there more straightaway hitting now than in former years?
4. Do you use straightaway hitting with no outs?
5. Do you use straightaway hitting when one run behind or a tie score?

BUNTING–SACRIFICE

1. Do you consider bunting a very important part of the game?
2. Do you use the sacrifice bunt in close games with no outs?
3. Do you usually bunt down third base line with a man on first? With a man on second?
4. Do you sacrifice a man to third base so that he can score on a long fly?

THE BUNT-AND-RUN

1. Do you consider the bunt-and-run a good play in baseball?
2. Exactly what is the bunt-and-run?
3. Do you use the bunt-and-run with a fast man on first base?
4. Do you use the bunt-and-run in a close game?
5. Do you use the bunt-and-run when a couple of runs ahead? Or behind?
6. If the batter is only a fair hitter is it advisable to use the bunt-and-run instead of the hit-and-run?

BUT DO THEY DO IT?

That ought to be enough to give the baseball squads in college a few days thought. Most of the more experienced amateurs could answer these questions. My idea is not to have them say what is right, but do they do it?

If they will check up and find whether the club has been paying attention to these things it will be a lot of help. A good idea is for the team to get together after a game that has been lost—or won, for that matter—and review it to see how many important points they have overlooked.

I hope this is not too technical for the average fan. If he, even, will try to figure out the answers to these questions he will be able to understand a lot of things on a ball field that always have been a mystery to him. Instead of razzing players for what may look like a stupid play, he will appreciate the fact that perhaps it was a well intended play that happened to go wrong. A ball player should never be criticized for doing what he knows to be the right play. For instance, nothing looks more stupid than a squeeze play that fails to go through and nothing gives quite so much of a thrill as one that works out as planned.

There is a marked difference between the sacrifice play—bunting to advance a runner with the chances of the batter being thrown out—and the bunt-and-run play.

The bunt-and-run play is another form of the hit-and-run, with the difference that the batter bunts instead of hitting hard. In other words, the runner starts with the pitcher's swing on the bunt-and-run. On the sacrifice, he may wait to see that the ball is laid down.

The answers to the first block of questions are almost obvious. The main thing for an amateur team is to see that they are done.

Take Time for Sizing Up

All good ball clubs should play the waiting game at the beginning. It gives them a chance to size-up the pitcher, a chance for him to put himself in the hole if he happens to be a little wild.

At the same time, it is a good policy to hit the first ball now and then. That upsets the pitchers.

A man like Mathewson or Miner Brown, for instance, would make suckers out of a whole ball club if they started out waiting on him and kept it up steadily. He would flap that first one right over the plate every time and put the batter in the hole. To stop that a team naturally would have to take a crack at the first one often, so as to make the pitcher change his mind. It works both ways, the result depending upon which is the smarter, the batter or the pitcher.

In past articles I have frequently referred to pitchers as being wonders on outguessing the batters. A good guesser has his chance when a club starts its waiting tactics. If he can tell when they will wait, and when they won't, he can beat them. That is what I mean by a good guessing pitcher.

The question as to whether there is more straightaway hitting now than formerly is merely a matter of observation. Of course there is more straightaway hitting. It is due to the lively ball. Batters have much more chance of hitting that lively ball safe than they have of fooling somebody with a bunt. As a result bunting is not nearly such a highly developed art as it was a few years ago. The same thing can be said of base running.

As to whether a batter should bunt toward third or first depends largely upon the situation. If there is a runner on second, he should certainly bunt toward third. That draws the third baseman and puts it up to the shortstop to cover—not an easy job. With a man on first it is optional. As a rule it is best to draw the first baseman off the bag if possible and make it hard to get the batter. The second baseman would have to cover. Often he also goes after the ball and throws the whole defense out of kilter.

What Do You Know
of the Hit-and-Run?

● ● ●

Continuing what I have decided to call my examination papers, I would like the amateur ball clubs now being organized in the colleges and on the town lots to get together and study the following group of questions. Also I would like some of the fans who are inclined to roast ball players on the spur of the moment to look thse over.

THE HIT-AND-RUN

1. Is the hit-and-run the most important offensive play in baseball?
2. Which is more successful in college ball, hitting behind the runner or ahead of the runner? In professional baseball?
3. Does the base runner get the same lead and start in a clean steal?
4. Is it advisable to hit-and-run with no outs and a close score? Not close?

5. Do you hit-and-run with one or two outs, close score? Not close?
6. Do you hit-and-run with a man on first and third?
7. Do you ever hit-and-run with a man on first and second ?
8. Do you ever hit-and-run with a pitcher on base?
9. Is the best time to hit-and-run when you have the pitcher in the hole?

Generally speaking the answer to most of those questions should be yes. Some of them, though, are open to discussion. It is that discussion that I am trying to encourage. Nothing gets a ball club or any other business as far along as an intelligent discussion of the problems that will have to be solved.

I submitted that set of questions to the boys at Carnegie Tech and you would be surprised to know that a large percentage of them answered them correctly.

One of them answered: "I know the answer ought to be 'yes' but you have asked if we do these things that we ought to do. The answer to that is often 'no.'"

While good hard common sense should be used in deciding whether to hit-and-run, it must be done sometimes as a surprise. I might explain that big league batters usually hit behind the runner for the simplest reason that they are skillful enough to do it. Hitting behind the runner means that if a runner is on first base, we'll say, the batter gives him the signal to start and he then hits the ball between first and second—behind the runner. That is a big point in the play. If the ball is hit through to right field the base runner can go all the way to third. If the ball goes into left he is likely to be stopped at second.

MUST BE SURE OF DIRECTION

Players, to work the hit-and-run successfully, must be men who are pretty sure of hitting the ball in the direction indicated. Many of them cannot hit into a certain field. As a rule ball clubs arrange their batting order so that the star hit-and-run men will be together and near the top of the list.

Willie Keeler and John McGraw were great hit-and-run men. In fact their club, the old Orioles, first made it a successful stunt. Kid Elberfeld was a good hit-and-run man. So was Miller Huggins. I never saw a better one than Fred Clarke. Claude Ritchey, though not a heavy hitter ordinarily, was very good at the play. Ty Cobb is a wonder at it. The former Boston Red Sox had it down pat. The hit-and-run, I think, is an ideal offensive play for college teams.

I leave the rest of the questions open for discussion. If any amateur is interested and can't find a ready answer just ask any major league ball player.

THE SQUEEZE PLAY—SINGLE AND DOUBLE

1. Is the squeeze play a good play in modern baseball?
2. Do you use the squeeze play with no outs, with a weak hitter? Good hitter?

3. Do you use it with one out and a weak batter? Good batter?
4. Do you advise the runner to wait until the pitcher is delivering the ball or to break as in stealing home?
5. Do you advise bunting to first or third base?
6. Why isn't the squeeze play used more in big league baseball?

I think I have given the younger player a few posers there. All of them, though, are like the first reader to the recruits after they have been in the league for a month. The answers to those questions are all based on common sense.

GRIFFITH GIVEN THE CREDIT

For the benefit of those who may not know definitions, the squeeze play is a runner starting for home as the pitcher throws to the batter. The batter bunts the ball. The runner is so close that there is no chance of getting him at the plate. Often, in the confusion, the pitcher also fails to get the batter at first.

This play came into general prominence with the New York Americans nearly twenty years ago. Clarke Griffith was often given credit for starting it. I don't know whether that is true. All the clubs used it, and with great effect at first.

I have asked why the big leagues do not use it oftener. The answer to that is that if they use it frequently the opposition would expect it. Any good pitcher can beat the squeeze play if he is looking for it. In fact, it was impossible to work the play on some pitchers.

A fan who read a previous article has asked me to give my opinion as to the best method of beating the squeeze play. If the batter is right-handed the only sure method for the pitcher is to throw directly at the batter's chest. That will keep him from hitting the ball and when he backs off the catcher will have a free hand and open in space in which to touch the runner as he slides in. If the ball is pitched outside—away from the batter—the catcher may be turned around so that he cannot whirl and touch the runner.

Christy Mathewson used to say that he could beat the squeeze play any time he kept his eye on third base. If the pitcher looks at the bag as he makes his swing he can see whether the runner has started. If he has started, all the pitcher has to do is pitch the ball high, outside or at the batter—anything to keep him from hitting it. If the batter misses the ball the squeeze play always looks ridiculous.

It was practically impossible to work the squeeze play on Alexander. The squeeze play is great for a surprise, but as a regular stunt it falls down. When it does fall down nothing in all baseball looks more stupid.

Do You Know What's Worth Rooting For?

• • •

As a conclusion to my baseball examination papers I present the following for study by the amateur ball teams this spring. A close study and discussion of them I feel sure will help.

STEALING BASES

1. Is the art of stealing bases on the decline?
2. Does the success of stealing lie chiefly in the lead and quick start or in speed?
3. Is stealing third advisable with none or one out?
4. Do you use the double steal with none or one out?
5. Has the half-balk motion of pitchers interfered with stealing?
6. Is the throwing of catchers more speedy and accurate?
7. Is it easier to steal third than second?
8. Have pitchers improved in holding runners on bases?
9. Do you advise stealing home? If so, when?

The answer to the first question, of course, is yes. This decline is due largely to the chances of hitting the lively ball safely. They are greater, I believe, than the chances of stealing successfully.

It is not my purpose to answer all these questions, thereby killing what interest they may have. For the benefit of the fan who is not so expert, however, I will explain that the stealing of third is, or should be, easier than stealing second. Many ball players contend that no man ought to be thrown out stealing third at any time. It is all in the start. An experienced ball player instinctively knows his own speed and is a good judge of distance. Therefore, if he has enough start to steal third he ought to steal it. With a good lead they can't throw him out. If he hasn't sufficient start then he ought not to steal. Ninety times out of a hundred, when a runner is thrown out stealing third it is a matter of bad judgment. Any skillful base runner can time the play exactly.

LIVELY BALL CHIEF FACTOR

Of course the pitchers and catchers both have improved but not enough to cause the present decline in base stealing. Most of that can be laid to the lively ball.

1. Is the single delayed steal a good play? Double?
2. Is the proper time for the man on first to start when the catcher is in the act of returning the ball to the pitcher? Or just when the catcher is actually throwing it to the pitcher?
3. Do you have a man stealing second go hard and then hold up near second, giving the man on third a chance to score when there are runners on first and third?

The delayed steal is a very tricky and a very effective play at times. It is called delayed because the runner does not start until the catcher has the ball—the ordinary steal starts with the pitcher's throw to the catcher. If the runner can start the exact moment when the catcher is letting the ball go back to the pitcher it will succeed often. It then takes two throws to get the runner, and the catcher's throw to the pitcher is never as fast as from the pitcher to the catcher. The delayed steal also has the element of surprise.

SUBSTITUTE PINCH-HITTERS

1. Is substituting pinch-hitters important in offensive baseball?
2. Would you substitute a pinch-hitter for a pitcher who is going all right at the middle of the game?
3. Do you believe in shifting your line-up according to left- or right-handed pitching?
4. Give a code of signals that could be used in offensive baseball.
5. Which do you consider the more important, a strong offense or a strong defense, including pitching?

6. Have the new rules on pitching hurt the effectiveness of pitchers in league ball? Actually? Psychologically?
7. Has the rule compelling the catcher to stay in the box until the pitcher has delivered the ball helped the offense? Has it prevented intentional passing of batters?
8. Is there as much inside baseball used today as in former years?

What Simple Signs Mean

These questions, I realize, open up a wide field of discussion. The opinion of any one man cannot decide them.

For instance, I do not believe in shifting a line-up for left- or right-handed pitching. At least I believe a team ought to be constructed so that such a shift would not be necessary. We never thought of such a thing in the old days. A good batter ought to be able to hit any kind of pitching. Still, there are very able managers who do make these shifts. There are critical moments, I admit, when it is a good thing. But as a general principle I do not believe in it.

That the uninitiated may understand my question on a code of signals, let me explain that all ball clubs have one. I have asked this question in the hope that amateurs will make theirs simple. Any complicated set of signals is worse than none at all. If a batter wants to signal for the hit-and-run and a simple sign is to rearrange his cap, rub the end of his bat, tap the bat on the heel of his shoe—any of those will do. As good a signal as any for stealing is simply for the coach at first base to tell the man when to go. Some teams use words instead of signs. We still laugh about the Boston manager who use to give the signal for stealing by yelling "Red Leary, the bank robber."

McGraw and Clarke always used very simple signals. I have seen McGraw merely indicate with his hands, while sitting on the bench, what he wanted the runner to do. Above all an amateur team should never have complicated signals. The signs as we call them can't be studied in baseball as they are in football—by a series of numbers.

As to the offensive side having an advantage by the catcher being forced to remain in his box until the ball is delivered, the result is an open question. The rule was intended to prevent the pitchers purposely passing batters. It certainly has been a failure in that respect. It is no trouble for the catcher to step out of the box after the pitcher has turned loose the ball. He can catch most of the pitch-outs without getting out of his box.

Personally I do not believe there is as much inside ball used today as in former years—simply because it is not necessary. With a lively ball to hit the batters are inclined to take a sock at it. Straightaway hitting is much more in vogue than it ever was.

I have intended these questions seriously. I felt that any narrative of baseball as told by me would not be worth while if I could not be of help to the coming players. If by these questions, which I have prepared very carefully, I have done any good, then I feel somewhat repaid. I want to see baseball develop and improve because I love it. I would like to see other young players have an easier time at the start than I did. They can do it by heeding the experiences of others. If they are ambitious to be professional ball players, then it is their duty to study their profession as a life work. If they don't they will be bushers in the end of their days. And that goes for men in any other profession. There is no secret about it. The key to success is hard work and application. Unless that work is enjoyable it won't count.

How the Game Can Be Strengthened

• • •

It is my opinion that any man who has given thirty years of his life to baseball has not wasted his time. He has contributed considerable to his country. That gives me a lot of satisfaction. I hope that all ball players will feel the same. By taking their profession seriously and giving as much as possible to the entertainment of the public and the encouragement of young boys to take up sport, they are sure to feel that way when they are about to retire and can look backward for reflection. I don't know of any profession in which I could have done as well as in baseball. It has been my only education. Without its opportunities I would not have been able to appreciate my own country as I have.

After considerable thought I am convinced that the game of baseball has done as much toward the amalgamation of races, toward Americanization, as any one factor in American life. It can do more.

Probably you have noticed that in the great cities like New York and Chicago, where the foreign population is large, the proportionate attendance at ball games is smaller than in cities more solidly American. For instance, a city like Cleveland will draw almost as many people to see a winning ball club as New York City, and it has about one-fifth the population.

Baseball people have overlooked many opportunities. They must look forward in the future. That foreign population is a great field. It has been suggested that the powers in baseball should start a movement looking toward Americanization by educating these foreign people into a love for baseball. Wherever they have a chance they take it up very quickly. I have seen little Italian boys trying to play baseball

183

the first year of their arrival simply because they saw the American boys doing it. In a short time they had the American spirit. Without that spirit, they are Americans in name only.

Now if the baseball people would cooperate with the public playgrounds associations in the various cities, and with the Americanization societies, I believe a scheme could be worked out by which great good could be accomplished for the new citizens, and also for the country. You can bet that whenever a foreign boy becomes a baseball fan he immediately becomes an American. It gives him the real idea of what America means.

Suppose, for instance, the big leagues should go into the playgrounds movement by contributing one experienced veteran ball player to conduct the games and instruct the little fellows at each public outdoor gathering place. In a very short time more playgrounds would be needed. It would start a general movement toward the outdoors and toward sport. The baseball people would be repaid tenfold by the number of fans developed and by the development of new ball players.

In this concluding chapter of my memoirs I would also like to indorse the plan suggested by John Heydler, president of the National League, looking toward the founding of a college for professional ball players.

Such a school, I believe, would pay the leagues, as well as the young ball players eager to enter the procession. There is no reason why we should not have a school for ball players just the same as we do for actors, for lawyers and other professions.

My suggestion is similar to that of Mr. Heydler in that the school should be to big league baseball what West Point is to the Army. Without a West Point our army would suffer for the lack of trained officers. It is just as necessary to league baseball that its players be trained and possessed of all the knowledge that men who have gone before can give them.

The methods in the past have been honest and sincere but sort of haphazard. The popularity of the game has really outgrown its system. Can you imagine what it would mean to the major leagues to have a college turning out from thirty to forty skilled players every year? Also, can you imagine how hard a young fellow would work

John A. Heydler was a government printer in Washington in the 1880s. His interest in baseball led him into umpiring and later sportswriting. He became secretary to National League president Harry Pulliam and interim president after Pulliam's suicide. Heydler was secretary-treasurer under President John K. Tener and succeeded Tener as National League president in 1918. Heydler was not very energetic in investigating scandal or in opposing league owners, but he was innovative in his thinking. He supported the selection of Judge Kenesaw Landis as Commissioner of Baseball in 1920, helped establish the Baseball Hall of Fame, and proposed the designated hitter as early as 1929. After resigning as president in 1934, he served as National League chairman of the board until his death in 1956. (George Brace Photo Collection)

to win a diploma from that school if he thought it a genuine stamp of approval and appointment or assignment to some major league club?

COLLEGE HELP TO GAME

The young player in the past, by force of circumstances, has been compelled to get most of his baseball education and training by his own efforts. The managers haven't the time or the inclination to spend several hours every day correcting the faults of the young substitutes and recruits who sit on the bench merely waiting for an opportunity to show what they can do. Often I have looked at their eager eyes from the field. I could almost feel that they were hoping to see some old fellow drop out so that they would have a chance. That is but natural. I reckon young officers in the Army, and in the police, look forward to the time when some veteran will be retired. It is their only chance for advancement.

I have known ambitious young ball players to shrivel up and lose their pep through lack of activity on the diamond. Sitting on the bench day after day and month after month is no easy job.

Now suppose we had a college founded and endowed by the big leagues and with well-known star players as professors or instructors—wouldn't that be a great place to send these youngsters that now sit on the bench? The clubs would be able to pay their tuition in what they would save in expenses. They could call them in when needed. The youngsters would have a chance not only to study the fine points of the game, but to put them in practice every day, right under the eye of men who knew their business.

A school like this would also give the old ball player something to look forward to. He could go there in dignified retirement and be an instructor. It would not be necessary for him to be kicked down the ladder from one small league to another. If the playgrounds scheme also was put into operation dozens of veterans could be employed there.

THE GAME AND THE SPIRIT

At present the only future left to a big-league ball player is to become a manager or a scout. There are not enough jobs for all of them. As a result they have to go into some business for which, as a rule, they are fitted by neither training nor temperament. Some are fortunate enough, of course, to have saved their money and to have invested it intelligently. Those, however, are not in the majority.

I think it not only a duty but a matter of good policy for our leading citizens, in official position or in private life, to encourage the sport of baseball—all sports, for that matter.

When the boys came back from France I remember one young fellow telling me why Americans made such good fighters.

"A Frenchman told me," he said, "that the secret of our Army success was that Americans all liked to play."

By that he meant that when they were not actually in the line they were constantly playing some game, mostly baseball. At night they would have boxing matches. Always, though, they were ready to play and laugh and root for their favorites.

That trait in most all Americans, I believe, is due to the national love for baseball and other sports. The more sports we have the better country we will have. As our sports grow in quality they will grow into even greater popularity. History tells us that great races of people were sport-loving people.

That is why I am proud of having been a ball player.